CREATIVE MEMORIES

The 10 Timeless Principles Behind
the Company that Pioneered the
Scrapbooking Industry

Cheryl Lightle

Cofounder of Creative Memories

with Heidi L. Everett

McGRAW-HILL

New York Chicago San Francisco Lisbon
London Madrid Mexico City Milan New Delhi
San Juan Seoul Singapore Sydney Toronto

The *McGraw·Hill* Companies

1 2 3 4 5 6 7 8 9 10   DOC/DOC   0 9 8 7 6 5 4

ISBN 0-07-143961-7

McGraw-Hill books are available at special quantity discounts to use as premiums and sales promotions, or for use in corporate training programs. For more information, please write to the Director of Special Sales, Professional Publishing, McGraw-Hill, Two Penn Plaza, New York, NY 10121-2298. Or contact your local bookstore.

Product or brand names used in this book may be trade names or trademarks. Where we believe that there may be proprietary claims to such trade names or trademarks, the name has been used with an initial capital or it has been capitalized in the style used by the name claimant. Regardless of the capitalization used, all such names have been used in an editorial manner without any intent to convey endorsement of or other affiliation with the name claimant. Neither the author nor the publisher intends to express any judgment as to the validity or legal status of any such proprietary claims.

 This book is printed on recycled, acid-free paper containing a minimum of 50% recycled, de-inked fiber.

Library of Congress Cataloging-in-Publication Data

Lightle, Cheryl.
   Creative Memories : the 10 timeless principles behind the company that pioneered the scrapbooking industry / Cheryl Lightle with Heidi L. Everett.
      p. cm.
   ISBN 0-07-143961-7 (alk. paper)
   1. Creative Memories (Firm) 2. Selling—Scrapbooks. 3. Direct selling. I. Everett, Heidi L. II. Title.
   HF5439.S38.L54 2004
   381'.45745593—dc22

                                                                    2004009319

To our consultants around the world who make a difference in the way others remember, celebrate, and connect.
To our employees for sharing a love and dedication to our Mission.

* * *

To my personal board of directors:
My grandmother, Grace Elizabeth McCafferty Holloway, who instilled my personal values.

Lee Morgan, CEO of The Antioch Company, who provided a work environment where my personal values meshed and flourished to help make a difference in people's lives.

My son, Brad Lightle, who always seems to ask probing questions that hold me accountable to those values.

Cheryl Lightle

To my inspiration, my loves:
Branden and Brody, for keeping me principled, grounded, and always laughing.

JD Everett

Contents

Statement of Highest Purpose

We exist to serve human needs by making a difference in the way people remember, celebrate, and connect and to maintain a community of work that offers opportunities to prosper and inspires hope for the future.

Mission Statement

Creative Memories believes in and teaches the importance of preserving the past, enriching the present, and inspiring hope for the future.

We strive to reestablish the tradition of the photo-historian storyteller and the importance of photo preservation for future generations.

We offer quality photo-safe products and information that utilizes cutting-edge technology.

We provide profitable career opportunities for those who believe in and want to share the Creative Memories philosophy, values, and ethics.

We offer a successful company that provides joy, dignity, and pride for Creative Memories consultants and staff members.

Foreword

The late Larry Burkett had a quote that is one of my favorites. He said, "While the carpenter is building a house, the house is building the carpenter." I love that thought because of its application to Creative Memories. I immediately translated that quote to, "While we are building Creative Memories, Creative Memories is building us."

Creative Memories Cofounder Cheryl Lightle and I have come to realize that this process of building Creative Memories has done as much to our personal character as it has impacted the world with our message of preserving our lives in safe, meaningful keepsake albums. These guiding principles that you will soon read about gave us strength and direction in this character- and business-building process.

Have you ever considered that everything that happens to you through your business—the joys, the frustrations, and everything in between—really wasn't about "the business." Instead, those experiences were about "you the person." The circumstances of your business are helping you to develop strong character, integrity, and learning skills that will serve you in all areas of your life. Each of those trials, every victory, every setback, every thing is part of a much bigger picture to build you into the person you need to be to fulfill your role.

Ruth Barton once said, "We set young leaders up for a fall if we help them envision the things they can do before they decide the type of person they want to be." Cheryl and I decided early on that operating by our guiding principles and doing the right thing even when it was hard was worth more than bottom-line profit and our personal image. I hope that every reader of this book comes away with the same conviction to value the role of guiding principles to shape both the people and the business. Then, when those character-building moments come, you will have a foundation on which to guide your decisions.

So as you read along and contemplate each guiding principle, I hope you will embrace each one. I can guarantee that you and your company will become stronger.

Rhonda Anderson
Creative Memories Cofounder

Acknowledgments

While the Creative Memories guiding principles are document-ed and prevalent in the home office, the stories and examples that support their creation and application needed to be uncovered and shared. As with all accomplishments, this book would not have been possible without the contributions of the following team.

A special thanks to Dana Wilde for taking diligent notes and pre-serving the Creative Memories history in the first years of operation; Mark Mizen for driving down the details as you edited; Ron Armes for unquestioned freedom to pursue this project; Amy Dahl, Jill Melby, and Monica Schifsky, for letting this project fall into the "other duties as assigned category." I appreciate your feedback.

To Donya Dickerson at McGraw-Hill for taking a chance, remain-ing calm, and gently guiding us through the process.

To Rhonda Anderson, Jeff Grong, Leilin Hilde, Susan Iida-Pederson, Lyn Johnson, Alan Luce, Asha Morgan Moran, Lee Morgan, Vicki Morgan, and Carol Ramke for your stories.

And, finally, to Cheryl Lightle, for your candid approach to the interview and editing process and for letting me into your personal and professional lives. Your secrets are safe with me. Perhaps another book is in order?

Heidi L. Everett

Introduction

I t all started with a chance phone call.

January 18, 1987, Cheryl Lightle, who was overseeing sales and marketing at the struggling Holes-Webway company, answered an after-hours phone call to take a message from a mail-order customer. On the other line was Rhonda Anderson, a Montana homemaker and mother of four. Cheryl knew that what was behind this woman's enthusiasm was the key to turning the company around. That call, which you'll learn all about in this book, inspired a vision that changed the way people remember, celebrate, and connect. That call gave birth to a multibillion-dollar industry, a tradition, a cherished way of life. That call lead to the founding of Creative Memories.

Today, Creative Memories has more than 90,000 independent sales consultants around the world who teach millions of people to preserve their special stories in safe, meaningful keepsake albums each year. Creative Memories consultants do not offer products and services from a store. They do not have a fixed retail location. Instead, consultants teach memory preservation through the direct-selling distribution model, which means they work one-on-one or in small groups of six to eight people in homes around the world. In 2002, more than 3 million people learned how to create keepsake scrapbook photo albums in the Home Classes (or "parties") and workshops taught by Creative Memories consultants.

In addition to the success of this direct-selling organization, Creative Memories was a catalyst for the formation of a multibillion-dollar retail scrapbooking industry. While Creative Memories was soaring through its tenth year, three mainstream national scrapbook magazines were founded and mom-and-pop retail shops not affiliated with Creative Memories started appearing in shopping centers all over North America. In 2003, larger retailers like Archivers and Recollections (founded by craft retailer Michael's Stores) opened stores devoted solely to scrapbooking. The December 28, 2003, the New York Times reported that the retail industry was estimated at $2 billion. That figure is expected to grow 40 to 80 percent in the next 5 years, the Hobby Industry Association states in the article.

Despite the emergence of direct retail competition in the scrapbook industry in the late 1990s and today, Creative Memories continues to grow and thrive as a direct-selling organization. Sales at the end of 2003 reached approximately $400 million retail worldwide.

This all started with a phone call.

Not bad for the little girl who wanted to be a cowboy.

HUMBLE BEGINNINGS

In order to understand what a great accomplishment this is, it's important to know the inspirational story of Creative Memories' Cofounder, Cheryl Lightle. Cheryl Lytle spent most of her adult life living within 1 hour of where she was born in Springfield, Ohio. Her first introduction to direct selling happened one summer in her neighborhood.

A traveling salesman showed up on the block one day with a horse and some cowboy wear and asked if anyone wanted their picture taken on the horse for a small fee. Cheryl jumped at the chance, loving the way she looked on that horse with the cowboy hat and vest. That experience had a lifelong impact on her. It inspired her to want to be a cowboy. And it showed her the power of direct selling as a means of reaching out to others.

But Cheryl's dream of riding off into the sunset on her trusted horse was short lived. In those days, girls' options were to be a housewife, a teacher, or a nurse. Cheryl recalls, "I knew I couldn't be a nurse, so I thought about teaching and changed my dream. I could picture myself in a 'far off' place—like Columbus or Cincinnati—with stacks of paper. I knew that would be the symbol that I had 'arrived.'"

Cheryl did, indeed, arrive; although, she didn't follow the path she had planned. Her humble beginnings and propensity to survive difficult situations laid the foundation for the guiding principles that would one day help build the company that pioneered the scrapbook industry.

To understand just how inspiring Cheryl is as a leader, it's important to know the key details about her own story and her start as a businesswoman.

Cheryl's parents divorced when she was 10. For a short time, Cheryl, along with her mother and her two brothers, moved in with her grandparents down the street. Cheryl took care of her brothers while her mother worked 40 minutes away. On Saturdays when her mother worked overtime, Cheryl would take the city bus to go pay the water and electric bills downtown.

Cheryl was a shy little girl, self-conscious of her tall, lanky frame and crooked teeth. She would often hide behind the couch when company would come to visit. The shyness was not overcome when her family moved to Fairborn, Ohio, before she was in seventh grade, and Cheryl had to acquaint herself with a new school and new friends.

In high school, Cheryl spent summers taking care of her grandmother in Washington Courthouse, Ohio, after her grandfather died. During her senior year, Cheryl moved in with her grandmother to take care of her full-time. While Cheryl loved caring for Grace, she was away from her own mother and two brothers, and, again, she had to learn to adjust to new surroundings and new people. On weekends, her mother and brothers would come to visit.

Cheryl Lytle married Ron Lightle one week after her eighteenth birthday. (She often jokes that it must have been destiny because the names were so similar.) When they moved into their first place, Cheryl looked for work to help pay the bills. Because she had no driver's license and no car, she had to find a job that was along the bus route.

For 5 years, she'd ride the bus to Dayton or Fairborn to work at a bank. When their first son, Brad, was born, Cheryl quit her job to raise children. "I believe raising kids to be good people—good citizens—is a worthwhile thing to do," Cheryl says. "We can't just send people out into this world without them knowing how to be good people. So that is where I focused my energy: my children."

After Brad, came Shelly and Rob. And throughout their childhood, they baked a lot of cookies and decorated cakes. Cheryl also sewed Halloween costumes for the kids. The memories of their childhood are fond ones for Cheryl. "I am proud to say I was able to walk all of my children to school on the first day each year. I remember when my youngest started kindergarten, I was out there with my camera, and he kept shouting, 'Mom, will you stop that!' That moment foreshadowed what was to come in my life with Creative Memories."

In addition to being available for her children during the elementary-school years, Cheryl is proud of the community outreach the kids were exposed to.

Cheryl's involvement with the church's Fish group provided the greatest impact on her and the kids. They had the Fish food shelf in their basement. They would assemble food packages for needy people in town. Then, they would load the food in the second-hand car her mother gave them, and Cheryl and the kids would deliver the food.

"I remember so many of the stories of people we helped. One woman had a new baby, and the father of the baby refused to give money to feed it. We would deliver food to them each week, so the baby could eat," Cheryl remembers. "Another time, federal marshals came to our home for food. They had arrested some parents for welfare fraud and relocated five kids to live with their grandmother. She needed help feeding the kids, so they came to us.

"All of these experiences taught me how absolutely fortunate my family was and how vitally important it is to give back to those who may not be as lucky."

PERSISTENCE PAYS OFF

In the fall of 1979, Cheryl and Ron bought a new home. Their youngest child was in second grade, and it was time for Cheryl to look for a part-time job and earn extra income. She was looking for jobs at banks, since that was her only professional experience. Although, she often points out, "Managing young children, operating a household, and keeping the bills paid is as close to human resources, team development, and finance as you can get. You just don't have the dirty diapers."

At that time, Cheryl saw an ad in the paper for The Antioch Company in Yellow Springs, Ohio. The Antioch Company was looking for a secretary for the president. Since The Antioch Company was closer to Cheryl's home than Dayton, she applied. While the interview went well, Cheryl bombed the typing test. She remembers, "I did something like 27 words a minute with 12 mistakes. I thought to myself, 'Well, this just isn't going to work.'"

Although Cheryl was discouraged, she was determined to find work. On her way out, she stopped by the receptionist and asked if anything else was available. According to Cheryl, "I said I'd be willing to pack boxes, anything at all. The receptionist told me they were looking for a temporary person in accounts receivable while someone is out on sick leave. She called the department to see if they could interview me right then.'"

They did. And Cheryl did much better on the math tests. She was hired.

That one extra effort on Cheryl and the receptionist's part opened the door for Creative Memories to be a reality. And the persistence and risk taking Cheryl demonstrated that day was a trademark of her work ethic and performance throughout her career with The Antioch Company.

Did her transition into the world of work outside the home come easily? No. Cheryl recalls, "After my second day of work with The Antioch Company, I didn't want to go back. I learned that after my interviews, one employee said not to hire me because she didn't like me. Jokingly, my future boss said, 'I'm going to hire her because I like redheads.' The other person responded, 'Yeah, but did you see her roots?' I just didn't feel like I fit into the environment and that I was being judged. After two days, all I had there was a coffee cup and some papers on a desk, so nobody would miss me. I did go back, though, and never regretted it."

From 1979 to 1984, Cheryl worked in accounts receivable, learning everything she could along the way about industrial revenue bonds, cost of inventory, and more. As she recalls, "We accounted for everything right down to square inches of excess foil for imprinting."

Then, in 1984, the company needed a new phone system. The investment would equal 30 percent of the company's annual profits. Cheryl was asked to review the 13 proposals submitted and make a recommendation of which vendor and system to select.

She recalls, "Suddenly, there I was, Cheryl who'd started out as a $3-an-hour accounting clerk, face to face with the president of the company. I'd only seen him in the hallways, and he was asking me to do something I'd never done before. I waded through the proposals, too committed to turn back. I was so far out of my comfort zone that I needed the Concord to get back."

Her recommendation was quite unorthodox. She said the proposals were too large of a financial investment, and she asked if it would be okay if she did the installation herself. Cheryl went to classes and became a certified Mitel phone technician in November 1984. She ultimately was responsible for maintenance of the system. Cheryl says that experience changed people's perception of her, "Offering to become a phone technician sort of catapulted me into a different playing field."

Shortly thereafter, Cheryl ended up in the original position she applied for, executive assistant to the president. In that role, her initiative and persistence continued. Production planning and the employee stock ownership plan were turned over to her as well as some additional accounting duties. She also assisted with acquisitions. Cheryl recalls, "Our chief financial officer used to call me a junior accountant. He said I knew just enough to be dangerous. Years later when Creative Memories became a $400 million company in 2003, he said I had graduated."

In August 1984 as Cheryl's career was taking hold, she and Ron divorced. While she had enjoyed work as a means of professional fulfillment, her focus shifted to that of having to earn a living.

When Antioch went to close the purchase of the Holes-Webway Company in November 1985, Cheryl went along for administrative support. Oddly enough, nobody—from the bankers and lawyers on down——thought to bring a check to buy out the controlling stock of the company. While the group was sitting around the boardroom table discussing the situation, Cheryl raised her hand and said she brought her checkbook and would be willing to write a personal check if Antioch would quickly transfer the $1,676 into her account, so the check would clear. Everyone agreed to the idea, and a handwritten transfer request was faxed back to Yellow Springs to ensure the funds were placed in Cheryl's personal account as quickly as possible.

These are fun stories to share from our company history. More importantly, they illustrate how Cheryl has not been afraid to take risks, to learn new things, and to be persistent in her work. That persistence paid off, and in January 1986, Cheryl was transferred to St. Cloud, Minnesota, to oversee the buyout and transition of Holes-Webway into The Antioch Company family. After 11 years as a stay-at-home mom with no formal education, Cheryl was being asked to bring a newly acquired company out of bankruptcy.

Antioch CEO Lee Morgan had this to say about Cheryl's move to St. Cloud, "It was a harsh January in 1986 when Cheryl left the only world she had ever known and moved to Minnesota, driving alone in a U-Haul truck, pulling her old, faithful Chrysler. This is a woman whose career prior to 1979 was homemaking and volunteer work. A person who had not been outside of the Midwest. A person who had not been outside of her home state. Yet when we wanted someone to move to Webway to represent the Antioch corporate culture, to help pull Webway back from bankruptcy and protect our investment, Cheryl was my first choice.

"Besides her penchant for taking on new challenges, there are three qualities which have contributed to Cheryl's success. First, she has vision. Second, she is tenacious. And third, she trusts her intuition. I know of no business school or seminar which teaches these qualities."

By May 5, 1987, a little more than a year after moving to St. Cloud, the bankruptcy was paid off. And Creative Memories was in the works.

In the coming pages, the history of Creative Memories will unfold as will the guiding principles that surround the day-to-day operations and business decisions of Creative Memories. Cheryl is credited with articulating the guiding principles and ensuring they are an integral part of the Creative Memories culture. The guiding principles, in their simplest form, represent treating people with dignity and respect. They can be applied to any work environment and any relationship, whether personal or professional. Many people believe the guiding principles are Cheryl's philosophies on life. Many believe they are a direct result of Cheryl's successes and challenges in life as a stay-at-home mom, wife, single mother, and volunteer. In essence, she experienced financial hardship, loss, and upheaval. She struggled to balance a work and home life. And she had to forego opportunities for herself that otherwise did not exist. She believed she had skills and talents to share, and she found ways to share them. Cheryl wanted other women to be able to do the same.

Creative Memories' Senior Executive Director Vicki Morgan joined us in September 1987, as our second consultant. She affirms that Cheryl's personal history impacted Creative Memories and the guiding principles. "Cheryl Lightle has always had a place in her heart for women. Cheryl believes women can manage a household, be a good mom and spouse, be involved in their community. So why not have them run a multimillion-dollar business?" Vicki said. "As a woman, Cheryl was married, had a family, divorced. She knew women had skills and talents that were untapped. She wanted to give them an opportunity."

And she did give women an opportunity. On July 4, 1987, Carol Ramke signed her consultant agreement and became the first Creative Memories consultant. Now, more than 90,000 Creative Memories consultants worldwide are successful home-based business owners regardless of their marital status, education, and prior work experience.

In addition, more than 1,000 employees of The Antioch Company operating units and Creative Memories business unit have found rewarding, enriching work supporting the Creative Memories sales force. As Cofounder Rhonda Anderson puts it, "In my heart of hearts, I know we could never do what we do without everybody giving their best to this cause. Creative Memories is more than just a job. We truly believe we can change the world and make a difference."

Cheryl is recognized as the leader of this glorious business known as Creative Memories. Yet she is known as a humble and gracious individual. As Cheryl recounts the story of Creative Memories and our guiding principles on the following pages, she does not seek out credit for the success of the organization, nor does she position herself as the reason for our existence. Yet the thousands of consultants, customers, colleagues, and staff who have met her or worked with her say otherwise.

"Cheryl really does care," said Carol. "When she talks to you, you feel like she really is just focusing on you. She's always been accessible—not just for me, but for everybody. If she didn't have that spark—that interest in people—she would've just took Rhonda's order and hung up when that phone rang in 1987."

Vicki affirms this when she says, "Cheryl Lightle sees the world in a big way."

And, Leilin Hilde, our third consultant who joined us in October 1987, had this to say, "I really appreciate Cheryl's quiet strength. In the early days, Creative Memories Cofounder Rhonda Anderson was our cheerleader. She was in the field teaching classes. She is the one we identified with. But Cheryl was in the background, humble. She laid down the guiding principles and framework that we didn't see. She did the legwork to build this business. She did it all with wisdom, character, and ethics. She did it quietly."

I, for one, am glad Cheryl had the interest and insight to learn more during that phone call in January 1987. And I know that sentiment is echoed by the 1,200 employee-owners of The Antioch Company, 90,000 Creative Memories consultants, and millions of people worldwide who have either made or received a completed, keepsake album. We are all better off because of Creative Memories and because of Cheryl's belief in possibilities.

Through my work as a writer, speechwriter, and company historian, I have seen first-hand how Cheryl believes in people, lives our mission, and keeps us focused on our consultants. All of these are wrapped up in the neat little package that is our guiding principles. The guiding principles are the greatest gift Cheryl has given us. And they are only part of the Cheryl Lightle legacy that will contribute to the long-term success of this organization.

As The Antioch Company CEO Lee Morgan put it, "It's difficult for me to introduce Cheryl Lightle without getting choked up. She has done more for this company than anybody else."

Heidi L. Everett

PART I

AN INSPIRATIONAL START

CHAPTER 1

IT ALL STARTED WITH THREE LITTLE WORDS

⸺✖⸺✖⸺

"In its most basic form, a wheel alignment consists of adjusting the angles of the wheels so that they are perpendicular to the ground and parallel to each other. The purpose of these adjustments is maximum tire life and a vehicle that tracks straight and true when driving along a straight and level road."

Retrieved December 31, 2003, from
Familycar.com's "Short Course on Wheel Alignment"

While it may seem odd to start a book about a direct-selling company with car talk, the metaphor of wheel alignment helps position the role of guiding principles in an organization.

Principles, by various definitions, can be basic truths, standards for conduct, or predetermined rules or policies. They can clarify rules of engagement in day-to-day work. Principles can outline why an organization makes the decisions it does. And, ultimately, they can provide clear direction and focus for strategic planning and daily decision making. If we think of principles like wheels on a vehicle, we understand that when they are properly aligned—or clearly articulated and practiced within an organization—they help the vehicle track straight and true. Without proper alignment of principles, we can veer off course, wasting valuable time and energy. Or, worse yet, we can decrease the life expectancy and effectiveness of our tires, or our organization.

In this book, we will address the Creative Memories guiding principles, how they came to be, and how they are used to keep us straight and true. Before we get into the guiding principles though, it's important to understand how the company started, grew, and became what it is today. And it's important to meet some of the inspirational people who helped it grow.

Creative Memories began, as we say, with "the call." Before we get to that legendary moment and the three little words that sparked our multimillion dollar industry, I should explain how I ended up on one end of that phone to begin with.

Our story actually starts in 1926 when two printing companies were founded—one in St. Cloud, Minnesota, which came to be known as Holes-Webway and the other in Yellow Springs, Ohio, which became The Antioch Company.

Holes-Webway was started by a gentleman named Wilbur Whipple Holes; friends called him Web. In 1938, Web designed the flex-hinge scrapbook album binding that was so innovative, people commonly referred to it as "Web's Way." The binding allowed albums to lie flat; it gave consumers the ability to add, remove, or rearrange pages in the album; and it created a much smaller gap between the pages so as not to interrupt the continuity of a double-page spread like D-ring or O-ring albums did. Driven by the flex-hinge binding and a new photo album business, Holes-Webway grew much faster than the Antioch Company, and by 1970 sales had passed $3 million. In 1970 Web died and was succeeded by his son. Though sales grew, peaking at $8 million in 1982, profits were elusive, and Holes-Webway declared chapter 11 bankruptcy in June of 1985.

Ironically, the founder of The Antioch Bookplate Company (later known as simply The Antioch Company), Ernest Morgan, was born in St. Cloud, Minnesota. The company he founded in Yellow Springs, Ohio, printed bookmarks, bookplates, and other sideline stationery items like journals and notepads. By 1970, The Antioch Company had sales of about $400,000 but was losing money. Thanks to a variety of events, The Antioch Company went into a period of sustained growth and profitability. By 1985, Antioch had sales of almost $11 million and was solidly profitable.

In an effort to save the Holes-Webway Company, the younger Holes invited every album manufacturer in the country to visit and buy out the company. No one was interested. The photo album business was perceived as a finite market in which competitors competed mainly on price.

It's not clear exactly why Antioch bought the Holes-Webway Company. I know Antioch was impressed by the albums, the manufacturing facilities, and the workforce. Still, the market was not looked at as favorable. Those who know CEO Lee Morgan, and Lee himself, admit Antioch purchased Webway because "He thought it would be fun." Lee has never really been motivated by money. Yes, he understands the need to have a strong, viable company. He believes, though, that we are here to make a difference and impact people's lives. The photo album business offered another opportunity to do that. Whatever the reason, in 1985 Antioch became the owner of a bankrupt photo album company with no reorganization plan.

That's where I come in. At the time, I was Lee's executive secretary. When we went to St. Cloud to buy out the controlling stock of Holes-Webway in November 1985, none of us thought to bring a check. So, I offered to write a personal check. The lawyers accepted it, and we quickly faxed a note to Antioch in Yellow Springs to make sure the money was put in my account.

My gallantry is probably what got me "rewarded" with the job offer of moving to St. Cloud to oversee the transition and get Webway out of bankruptcy. And I was honored that Lee trusted in me to translate the Antioch culture to Webway employees.

In January 1986, I moved to St. Cloud, Minnesota, to oversee sales and marketing at Holes-Webway. As the new kid in town, I spent many a subzero night bundled up in my apartment poring over customer letters from long-time Webway users who were having difficulty finding products during the bankruptcy. I was trying to figure out why consumer loyalty was so high. I knew there was a market niche there somewhere.

In January 1987, I was working after hours when the night bell informed me of an incoming call. While I didn't usually handle customer order calls, the phone just kept ringing and ringing and ringing. Customer service was closed for the night. And, we had no answering machine to pick it up, so I decided to.

On the other end was Rhonda Anderson, a Montana homemaker and mother of four. She had preserved her family memories in keepsake albums since she was 15. So, when her sister called and asked her to give a craft presentation on making keepsake albums to a local class for Mothers of Preschoolers, she reluctantly accepted. She thought everyone kept albums the way she did and that the participants would not be interested.

"When my sister called, I declined initially, saying I don't do crafts. The only 'hobby' I do is scrapbook albums, and everybody did scrapbook albums, so class attendees would be bored. But, I agreed to do it because I owed her for babysitting," Rhonda said. Thank goodness she did.

Rhonda immediately started to develop a handout outlining the importance of why everyone should have a photo album. They build self-esteem and a sense of belonging by identifying who we are, our family, our values, and way of life; albums are entertaining; they preserve family history. Her fourth reason was that if you spend the money on a camera, film, and processing, why wouldn't you put your pictures where you could easily look at them?

The morning of the class, Rhonda taught why everyone should have albums and how to make albums meaningful with documentation, memorabilia, and photos. She taught how to trim photos and add stickers to decorate empty space or cover up mistakes. Then she showed the class some of her own albums. The response was amazing.

"After the class, they rushed me, confessing that their family photos were in shoeboxes, dresser drawers, or in 'yucky' albums," Rhonda remembers. "Within minutes, I had orders for 40 photo albums just like mine and requests for me to teach my class to others. After teaching five more classes, it was obvious to me that not everyone had albums like mine, and that people needed help and encouragement to complete albums."

After Rhonda's presentation, she sought the advice of a lawyer friend to determine how to pursue the concept of teaching others to make keepsake albums. He encouraged her to call the Webway company and share her experiences. As Rhonda recalls, "He looked at me very seriously and said, 'Rhonda, every day I have people in here who have no hope. They want to walk out on their families and their jobs, everything. If only they had albums like these. Everyone needs albums like these.' His words were a huge validation for me. It was then that I knew we could save the world with a photo album."

Upon returning home from the lawyer, Rhonda found a postcard from Webway that she thought stated her favorite album had been discontinued. Not realizing it was after hours, she called the corporate office. Rhonda was bound and determined to let that phone ring because she needed 40 of those albums.

After several rings, I picked up the phone and said, "Thank you for calling Webway. I'm sorry, but customer service is closed. Can I take a message?"

Rhonda enthusiastically told me about her presentations and how she couldn't believe that people kept their precious photographs in shoeboxes. I was fascinated by the story and asked if I could call her back within a few days because I wanted to share what she was doing with our CEO Lee Morgan.

"Cheryl calls me and tells me about this woman from Montana and her scrapbook presentations," Lee remembers. "She tells me she's invited Rhonda to the home office to give a scrapbook presentation. I figured what could it hurt to have her come in and talk to employees."

Rhonda's initial presentation was to Webway employees in March, and their response was positive. One gentleman, our vice president of marketing, said after the presentation that his neck hairs stood up. I understood what he meant. I get goose bumps every time I see our mission in motion or hear about how we have positively impacted someone's life. I had goose bumps the first time Rhonda and I talked. There was something so right about our vision. So, I asked Lee if Rhonda could give another presentation to employees at The

Antioch Company in Yellow Springs. He agreed, and we scheduled more presentations to employees and others in June.

"I was skeptical but agreed to let Rhonda give a presentation to my friends—who are known as pretty stingy people," Lee says. "I knew she'd never get them to buy into the concept. The night of the presentation, Cheryl and I are standing in the kitchen and watching Rhonda pour her heart out about the importance of scrapbooks. I told Cheryl it would have little impact on the attendees.

"They proved me wrong when they swarmed Rhonda after her presentation," Lee admits. "They wanted to know more about creating scrapbook albums for their families. They bought every album she had. Rhonda actually sold albums to my friends."

In addition to the presentation Rhonda gave to Lee's friends, she also spoke to groups like the historical society, library association, and other general consumers we could pull together. These presentations were set up and scheduled by Lee's wife, Vicki Morgan. At the time, Vicki was a stay-at-home mom raising two kids. Prior to raising children, Vicki had been a teacher and salesperson. From time to time, she was hired by The Antioch Company for marketing and public relations activities.

"I thought the concept of scrapbooking was interesting," Vicki says. "I also knew that if Cheryl was responsible for it, it definitely would be interesting."

After each presentation, Vicki believed the concept was viable; however, each presentation was different from the one before it. Then, one night, Vicki came home and said to Lee, "Honey, we've been married 20 years. Our photos have graduated from shoeboxes to milk crates. We need to rifle through it all and work on our albums." And, she did just that.

"I saw the wisdom of capturing an entire life in albums, but I was overwhelmed," Vicki admits. So, she started working with her most recent photographs from January 1987 because "I knew where the photos were and could remember the details about them."

"As I worked on the albums, the kids would come in and out of the kitchen and say the albums were 'cool,'" Vicki remembers.

After the success of the scrapbook album presentations given in June, I asked Lee if we could pursue the idea. At that time, he uttered three short but profound words. He simply said, "Go for it."

Rhonda, Lee, and I then agreed to have Rhonda continue to give presentations in Montana to see what kind of feedback we got. Our vision was and still is that someday every household would have safe, meaningful keepsake scrapbook albums and that everybody's first instinct when they pick up their photos from the developer would be to get those pictures into an album.

Rhonda went back to Montana with one thing in mind: promoting keepsake albums at an upcoming home and garden show. She ordered 1,000 photo albums to sell at the event since 15,000 people were expected to be in attendance.

Even though Rhonda only sold 60 albums at the show and had 940 sitting in her garage, the enthusiasm she generated for teaching Home Classes gave me goose bumps. It gave Lee a headache from wondering, "What are we getting ourselves into?"

It only took Rhonda 5 months to sell those remaining 940 albums, and the interest that was generated was overwhelming. She was teaching five classes a week, and with each one she was more convinced of the positive impact albums had on the lives of people. Another lesson we learned was that the albums didn't simply sell themselves in a retail environment, which was illustrated at the home and garden show. Instead, it was the one-on-one and small group classes Rhonda taught in people's homes that really resonated with people.

In the meantime, I was busy learning more about an organization based out of Washington, D.C. that Lee had heard about called the Direct Selling Association (DSA). The DSA is a national trade association representing more than 150 direct-selling companies. Its mission is to protect, serve, and promote direct-selling companies and representatives and to ensure that the marketing of products and programs is conducted with the highest level of ethics and service to consumers. The DSA was hosting a conference, and I signed up to attend. I wanted to meet as many industry experts as I could to learn more about direct selling.

While I was familiar with the concept of direct selling as a customer of Tupperware and Mary Kay cosmetics and Rhonda was familiar with the sales side through her work with Tupperware and Shaklee nutritional supplements, the corporate-to-salesperson side of the business was not known to me. We needed to learn about setting up a career plan to compensate the sales force and about hostess programs; manufacturing; and distribution philosophies to the sales force, customers, and hostesses. There was so much to learn. And, I was not afraid to ask questions. In fact, one of my personal philosophies in life and in business is that you should never be afraid to ask anything. Alan Luce, now president of the direct-selling consulting firm Luce and Associates, realized this philosophy of mine early on in our business relationship.

"I first met Cheryl shortly after she joined the Direct Selling Association," Alan remembers. "Over the years, we'd talk about party-plan issues, policies, procedures, recruiting, distribution. The idea of scrapbooking did not come to me naturally. It was like, 'Gosh, I would not have known you could make a business out of memories and family tradition.' Cheryl proved otherwise. What I enjoy about Cheryl is she is totally open. She admitted she didn't grow up in this business. She'd say, 'Tell me in 30 words or less what you know.' Cheryl was refreshing, not defensive, and she asked great questions with penetrating follow-up. 'Why?' was her most frequent question. That honesty translated itself into an easy kind of leadership style."

The fascinating aspect of the DSA for me was the openness and willingness to share. Despite the perception of new direct-selling businesses being direct competition, the direct-selling corporations I met understood the importance of mentoring and helping newcomers. Success for any company in this industry raises awareness of our distribution model and provides success for others. Alan and the countless other direct-selling professionals I have met along the way were always patient with my questions, honest in their feedback, and encouraging. The relationships formed in our first years are still very strong. And, we are proud that Creative Memories has been able to return the favor by helping other new start-ups join the business by hosting them at our office for a day to meet and talk with our staff.

With our business model aligned with direct selling, it was time to start building our independent sales force, our field organization. Because of the interest generated by Rhonda's presentations, I decided it was time to get on the phone and contact another long-time Webway album customer who shared the same passion for albums as Rhonda and who might want to help teach presentations. That customer was Carol Ramke. Carol's mail-order letter to Webway, dated January 15, 1987, said:

> *I have been buying your albums since 1973 and have gotten my family to use them as well. At the present time and for about a year now I have been unable to purchase them or obtain information about them. I should have written sooner, but I am now to the last of my "spare" books. I do hope that you still make them.*
>
> *I would like to continue using them and would very much like to start an album for our 2-year-old and 5-month-old, as we have for their older sister. You do have a good product, and we certainly have the photo albums over the years to show for it.*

When Rhonda Anderson made the historical after-hours call to Webway to purchase albums on January 18, 1987, Carol's letter was still on my desk. And, when Lee uttered those three little words to pursue Creative Memories, I found Carol's letter and she is the person I called.

"Cheryl called me in June 1987, but I was on vacation," Carol recalls. "I thought it was just one of those usual sales calls. She started by saying, 'You don't know me, but my name is Cheryl Lightle. I'm with Webway.' I knew the name Webway. I had been using

Webway albums since 1973 and loved them. She called me back July 1, and on July 4, she got me."

I told Carol about Rhonda's presentations and asked if she would like a few weeks to think about joining our team. She didn't need a few weeks.

Carol remembers, "As we talked, my excitement grew. The timing was so neat. I had been an elementary education teacher and had been looking for something new. So, when Cheryl called me, I immediately said 'yes.' I agreed to get all my friends and family to come to a presentation. I called everyone I knew and said 'I'm starting a new business. You need to be my guinea pigs. Which night can you come?'"

Carol signed her consultant agreement July 4, 1987, and Creative Memories was officially born. She is with us today as one of Creative Memories' top field leaders. And, in one of her photo albums, she has a note I sent her in March 1988 that states, "I'm so glad I made that call to you. You have played such an important role in our company."

Then came our second consultant on September 22, 1987.

Vicki Morgan, you'll remember, had set up test presentations for Rhonda in Ohio. After evaluating the presentations, she began getting 20 years of family photographs into keepsake albums. In September 1987, she called me and asked if it would be okay for her to become a consultant.

"I got into this business because I thought it would be fun," Vicki says. "My degree was in elementary education, but I really wanted to be in sales. Creative Memories is a fortuitous blend of teaching and satisfying a 'creative or created' finished product and sales. I love working on my own albums, and I like making the money. It's instant gratification."

"When Cheryl and Rhonda recruited my wife to be the second consultant, I really thought, now what are we getting ourselves into?" Lee recalls.

Our third consultant was Leilin Hilde. Leilin's husband and Rhonda's husband were college roommates. Leilin learned of Creative Memories the summer of 1987 when the family was visiting the Andersons in Montana.

"My first impressions of Creative Memories were very exciting," Leilin said. "I remember listening to Rhonda talk about the company's mission, and I had goose bumps. Cheryl always talks about the importance of goose bumps. That is exactly what I felt.

"Prior to seeing Rhonda, I had never given much thought to my pictures. I bought albums, but never the same album twice. Creative Memories showed me the answer I never knew I had been searching for."

In 1988, Rhonda packed up her four young children and her husband into a van and set out on a 10-state cross-country marketing campaign to try and generate interest for our program. Creative Memories' first employee, Susan Iida-Pederson, was at the home office and she contacted local radio stations, hotels, cable shows, and newspapers, getting them to schedule Rhonda for their show, sometimes just hours before Rhonda and the van arrived in town. We told them about our incredible photo-preservation message and ground-floor opportunity.

By 1989, we had almost 100 consultants, and we continued to seek national and regional media coverage on the Nashville Network's American Magazine Program and others. Our big break came in March 1990 when Rhonda was on the Focus on the Family radio broadcast and magazine publication. This exposure generated 7,000 leads and the addition of 500 consultants.

As we continued to add consultants, we also came up with other essential elements of our business, such as product, catalogs, training materials, order forms, and membership in the DSA. We implemented a career plan in July 1990, so our consultants had a clear path for development and compensation. A career plan, in the direct-selling industry, indicates how a company will compensate a consultant for business activity. Consultants can earn commissions on their personal sales and the sales of their team members. They can also earn bonuses for training and developing new people on their teams. While every direct-selling company has a different career plan, all of them compensate for sales and team development. Prior to 1990, our consultants only earned income on their personal sales activity. The new plan offered compensation for their personal activity and for building a team.

When 1990 was through, I was able to share with Lee that our sales were over a million dollars wholesale.

And we were proud to announce to Lee when we had our first million-dollar month (in October 1993), million-dollar week (July 31 to August 4, 1995), and million-dollar day (in March 1997). Our goal is to be a half-a-billion dollar company by 2005.

Currently, we have more than 90,000 consultants in nine countries. We also have more than 1,200 employee-owners who work diligently each day at our home office, printing and packaging facility, and three manufacturing and distribution facilities. In 2002, we reached millions of people through the Home Classes our consultants taught. Sales in 2003 were approximately $400 million.

One might say we really did "Go for it" as Lee suggested. But, our success has not come without learning opportunities and challenges. The guiding principles and leadership lessons you will read about in the chapters ahead helped ground our explosive growth by giving us focus and direction.

Who could have predicted that one phone call would change our lives so dramatically?

CHAPTER 2

IT'S A PEOPLE BUSINESS

Creative Memories' tens of thousands of consultants are reaching people every day. They help others capture their stories in keepsake photo albums. While our consultants may be able to quantify the number of albums completed or memories captured, they cannot qualify the impact that those albums—those stories—will have on current and future generations.

Imagine for a moment that you came across an album created by your great grandmother. It shares letters that she and your great grandfather exchanged during courtship, with all the flirtations and admiration. It captures her hopes, dreams, and fears. Perhaps it shares her plans for having children and keeping a house. That album connects you with a woman you never met. It gives voice and depth to a woman you have only known as a two-dimensional image in old family photographs. That album helps define who you are and where you came from.

Our consultants help provide that connection, although they may never fully know the impact all the albums they have helped to complete will have on others who are yet to be born.

In this book, I frequently discuss the importance of relationships. A key part of a relationship is the impact we have on each other. We are all a step on the way to something grand, something good, and may never fully understand the true impact, the far-reaching effects of our actions. It has been said that when a butterfly flaps its wings on one side of the globe that that small action can start a hurricane on the other side. Consider yourself that butterfly for a moment. When you flap your wings, what will happen? As a leader, a coworker, a teacher, a friend, a family member, what type of impact do you want to have on others?

In Chapter 1, we explored the events that made Creative Memories the successful company it is today. Just as important as the events are the individuals who directly, or indirectly, helped the company grow. This chapter provides their inspirational stories.

In Creative Memories' history, many individuals helped plant the seeds that would one day be cultivated in that famous phone call with Cofounder Rhonda Anderson and me. And, I can only hope that they are able to look down on us and see the value and richness that they helped bring to people's lives.

They are truly inspirational.

BETTY CALLAWAY

My mother, Betty Callaway, and father divorced when I was 10. At the time, I was one of the few children in school who fell into the category of having a mom who "works." I've always been amazed by people who don't think stay-at-home moms work. As I always say, running a household and raising children provide some of the best on-the-job training.

My mother taught me so many things about surviving and thriving. She showed me how to be tough, strong, and independent. She taught me to work hard. And she never allowed any of us to have a "poor me" attitude. Of course, we all could have our moments; we just couldn't be consumed by them.

Most importantly, Mother shattered the myth that women can't make it on their own. The spirit and drive and survival skills that my mother demonstrated for my brothers and me come to mind every day when I hear stories from our Creative Memories consultants. These women are finding their own definitions of success on their own terms.

For the majority of Creative Memories consultants, they work less than 10 hours a week. And in that 10 hours they earn some extra spending money, they find a social outlet, and they engage in meaningful work helping others.

The 5 percent who make Creative Memories a full-time career choice are thriving as business owners in nontraditional ways. They are able to balance their personal priorities first; business priorities are second. As one of our top leaders, Executive Director Lyn Johnson, put it, "I don't even have an office. I run an 8 to 10 million dollar business from a table in my kitchen." By being a consultant, these women have time for their home, families, or whatever their priorities might be.

And, as colleagues, all of them challenge, support, and recognize each other. They grow together as public speakers, salespeople, business professionals, leaders, and mentors.

Every one of them has an inspiring story, just like my mother. Their drive, determination, and ability to enrich the lives of their family, friends, and communities inspire me to always give my best. And, the encouragement and belief they have in each other reinforces that which my mother always modeled.

The constant encouragement from my mother is what drove me to make the move to Minnesota in 1985. It was 1 year after my divorce. My life was in one of those midair moments where you let go of what is comfortable and hope you land on your feet. I wasn't going to fall flat on my face.

My mother was known for saying, "Do it while you can because someday you might not be able to." When my mother passed away in July 2001, a granite bench was donated in her honor alongside the pond at the Creative Memories home office. That quote is etched in the granite as a constant reminder to seize opportunities and take risks, even when they require you to step outside of the comfort of the familiar.

WEB'S WAY

An explosion and a book of matches were part of the historical chain of events that led to Creative Memories.

Things were going well in the 1930s for Wilbur "Web" Holes, an entrepreneur, publisher, and inventor, in St. Cloud, Minnesota. But, tragedy struck in 1938 when an adjoining business exploded, causing a wall to collapse on him. His back was fractured.

Web was known for his "never say die" attitude, and the injury didn't keep him down.

During his recuperation, he tried to help his sons save and display their matchbook collections. And, the "shoelace" bound scrapbooks he found for the project didn't meet with his standards. He felt they were impractical and primitive. He decided to develop a better scrapbook with a better binding. And he did.

That binding, known as the Flex-Hinge binding, allowed albums to lie flat, and it allowed album makers to add, delete, or rearrange pages in their albums.

People loved the quality and function of the album so much that they started to refer to it as Web's way of scrapbooking. And, in the late 1930s, limited quantities of Webway albums were produced. By 1945, Webway albums were available in the mass retail market through drugstores.

Web's inventiveness and commitment to quality created a loyal consumer following that I didn't fully understand when The Antioch Company purchased the bankrupt Holes-Webway Photo Album Manufacturer on November 14, 1985. I would soon realize and appreciate the value of Web's work.

When I moved to Minnesota in the winter of 1985, I was greeted by 8-foot snowdrifts and little to do. I had spent my entire life up to that point living within 15 miles of where I was born, so my move to the Midwest left me without most of my family, friends, and familiar places of comfort to retreat to. My oldest son was going off to college. My 15-year-old daughter came with me for a short time, and my youngest son stayed with his dad.

I spent many evenings at work poring over customer letters from people who were searching for Webway photo albums after they were removed from retail shelves during the bankruptcy. In fact, for over 20 years, Webway received 500 to 1,000 inquiries a month from customers. And the Webway staff kept the letters. They were proud of the consumer following. They were proud of their album quality. And when I joined the Webway team as vice president of marketing, they were quick to point out that those customer letters were one of our greatest assets.

They weren't kidding.

Some people searched for years to find the albums before contacting the manufacturer directly. And when people would write in, they wouldn't just order product. They would share their stories.

One woman, Brenda from New Mexico, had this to say:

> *A year ago I organized and redid all of our photo albums for the past 13 years. I used your Webway albums #W-35. I love them. I have been so thrilled with the quality of these albums that I want to continue using the same ones . . . I love these albums. In fact, I just purchased 5 of your albums to put them together for my children. Thank you for making such a fine product.*

What Brenda wrote was so typical of the day-to-day crop of new letters that came to our door. People loved the product. I know I have my favorite products and hate to see them go away. I get upset when they change my lipstick shade, but I don't take the time to call the company, express my concern, and seek out new options. I move on. This wasn't the case with Webway customers.

People felt an emotional connection to their photos because of the album quality. When they saw their precious photos displayed in mint condition, year after year, generation after generation, they were more than satisfied. They were wonderfully happy.

Web died on August 8, 1970, of a heart attack. Although I never had the opportunity to meet him, I do feel like his spirit lives on in the millions of completed, cherished albums that now grace the shelves and coffee tables of homes around the world.

I am personally grateful for his commitment to quality and innovation. I'm sure he had no idea at the time that his engineering genius would have such a profound impact on generations to come.

And I thank him for indirectly bringing Rhonda Anderson and me together and for indirectly leading me to our first Creative Memories Consultant, Carol Ramke.

We pay tribute to Web every day on our historic tour of the home office and facility in St. Cloud and in our commitment to quality when we produce the binding he invented.

ADA KANNING

Ada Kanning purchased her first Webway photo album from the Rexall Drugstore in Plentywood, Montana, in 1949. That simple act started the course that led her daughter, Creative Memories' Cofounder Rhonda Anderson, to that famous phone call. Since that first purchase, the Kanning family exclusively used Webway products—as Rhonda said, ". . . despite the difficulty in locating them."

Rhonda grew up with every picture that was ever taken of her and her siblings all neatly displayed in Webway albums with the appropriate journaling. Documentation included first and last names, dates, and places; the albums were history books.

Rhonda described Ada's commitment to preserving memories this way: "My parents were married when they were 18 and 19 years old. They had little money. Within 2 years they had two children: me and my brother, Jeff. My mother had splurged and purchased a Webway photo album when I was born, but when Jeff was born, money was really tight. Mom could not afford to buy a Webway photo album for him. Instead she chose to use a string-bound scrapbook that she had received as a shower gift. Mom's frustration with this string-bound album quickly grew; it wouldn't lie flat and within a few months the pages were tearing away from the binding.

"Life continued and just 1 year after Jeff's birth, my sister Lori was born. With three children now, money was really scarce. There was no way Mom was going to repeat her experience with the string-bound album, so she chose to cut her food budget and used the savings to buy photo albums. She was determined to provide all three of her children with the *best* photo albums for their memories."

When Rhonda turned 15, Ada decided it was time for her to begin preserving her own memories. Rhonda's first page chronicled a piano recital and included journaling and memorabilia, which are essential elements that we teach about today. The page even included a classified ad:

> *Capable high school student giving beginner piano*
> *lessons. Much experience and reasonable prices.*
> *Call and ask for Rhonda.*

Her entrepreneurial spirit was evident at such an early age! That business sense combined with a love for album making was the perfect blend for the direct-selling opportunity that would present itself in 1987. Her passion and commitment to preserving memories was evident in that first phone call, much like the customer letters that we had been receiving at Webway for decades.

What Ada taught was deeply engrained in Rhonda and served as the inspiration for Creative Memories' mission, product, and program. Ada also believed you could solve any problem by just working hard. She taught Rhonda to "just get to work." That strong work ethic was essential in Creative Memories' early days of operation.

Ada passed away January 6, 2002, and she is honored with a granite birdbath alongside our pond at the home office next to my mother's bench.

ERNEST MORGAN

Excess scrap paper inspired Ernest Morgan to create a community of work where all employees shared in the risks and rewards of a company.

The Antioch Bookplate Company was founded in 1926 by Ernest. He was an apprentice at the Antioch Press, the campus print shop at Antioch College in Yellow Springs, Ohio.

He and a fellow student-apprentice, Walter Kahoe, were concerned about the excess paper scrap generated at the print shop and decided to recycle it to make bookplates. Ernest did janitorial work in exchange for the use of the printing equipment after hours.

The first year, sales averaged a little over $2 a day. Then the dean of the college told Ernest, "Make up your mind that if the bookplate business hasn't started to pay by some certain date, say next January, you'll quit and take a job!" It never happened.

Ernest was offered a job at an established printing company and he turned it down to go into business for himself. The culture of his company was influenced by how he was raised. In an address to employee-owners just months before he passed away in 1999, Ernest told this story of his heritage and values:

> *My father was strong on caring and sharing . . . In his engineering practice in Memphis, he hired another young engineer to help him. The man worked out well, so Dad made him a partner.*

> *In time they hired another engineer, and Dad wanted to make him a partner too, but his original partner objected. "We've got a good thing. Why should we share it?" But Dad was the senior partner, so they took the man in.*

> *After a while they hired a fourth engineer, and he too worked out well, so Dad wanted to make him a partner. But then it was two to one—no more partners!*

> *Later, Dad was called to Dayton to head a vast flood control project. He started another engineering company. In those days workers were*

*housed in tarpaper shacks. But Dad cared about
the workers, so instead of tarpaper shacks, he
built five beautiful villages. They cost a lot more
than tarpaper shacks, but the quality and stability
of the work force were so high that it actually
saved money. Furthermore, the accident rate
was reduced by 85 percent.*

*Growing up in a family in which caring and
sharing was taken for granted as a way of life,
it is not surprising that I developed my own
company along those lines.*

*I ran the business as a community. When I hired a
new person, I took him or her on a tour of the office
and plant and gave permission to use the equipment
for personal printing or printing for non-profit organizations. In this community setting, the differences of
race, religion and color ceased to matter, and the
people were happy in their jobs. I recall one woman
who left to take a better-paying job but returned
shortly. "Money isn't everything!" she said.*

*I ran the business democratically. The difference
between my salary and the pay of my employees was
not large. And I recruited a committee of employees
to run the company, the "Operating Committee"
it was called. I was, of course, a member of the
committee, and sometimes my decisions were
overruled when they seemed unwise.*

*In 1970, when I was 65, I retired and turned the
management of the company over to my son Lee. He
was well-trained and carried forward the Morgan
family tradition of caring and sharing.*

The values of caring and sharing have truly contributed to our success. These fundamental values manifest themselves in our company's belief in its people and their ideas. This is part of The Antioch Company's Corporate Culture that is carried on to each of the business and operating units. It's this belief in people that told me I could make a difference when Lee asked me to move to St. Cloud. It is also this culture that made me feel comfortable talking to Lee about the concept of Creative Memories.

The role of corporate culture is hard to measure, but in our history a strong corporate culture has been critical since the beginning.

As Lee remembers his father's legacy, he says, "Business was a vehicle for him to be independent. Ownership was viewed as stewardship, not a right. There are several legacies of this general philosophy. First is our board of directors. Our board is composed of five outsiders, two members of management, and five employee-owners elected by staff. Two of the employee-owners are voting members. We are 100 percent employee-owned through an employee stock ownership plan (ESOP) that was started in 1979.

"Ideas for new product, programs, processes, etc., come from our employees every day—much like Cheryl shared her and Rhonda's vision for Creative Memories. And," continues Lee, "we have a program called IDEAS which stands for Improved Departmental Efficiency and Safety. Our employee-owners own what we do and proudly take stock in what happens on a day-to-day basis."

We will discuss all of these things in greater detail throughout this book. What is important to note at this time, however, is that the culture of sharing and caring that Ernest Morgan implemented in 1926 is invaluable to our organization. This culture resonated with me and ultimately gave me the comfort level to approach Lee about this vision that Rhonda and I had. And, the value of sharing and caring is a deeply engrained legacy of Ernest's that we still practice today.

As you can see, Betty Callaway, Wilbur Holes, Ada Kanning, and Ernest Morgan were four very distinct individuals living their own distinct lives. They couldn't have known that the encouragement, innovation, album-making tradition, and values they imparted on others would one day come together to ignite an industry, to cele-brate life, and to open opportunities for employees, consultants, and customers to remember, celebrate, and connect.

Never underestimate the influence you have on others now and for generations to come.

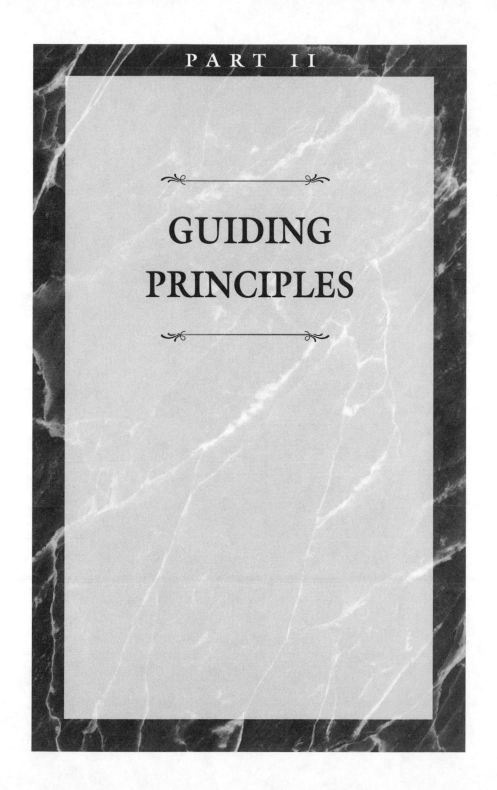

PART II

GUIDING
PRINCIPLES

CHAPTER 3

PUTTING PRINCIPLES ON PAPER

❧———————❧

Creative Memories Guiding Principles

1. *Operate from least to most.*

2. *Embrace the abundance mentality.*

3. *Keep the promise.*

4. *Make it easy.*

5. *Communicate clearly and concisely.*

6. *Protect the relationship.*

7. *Respect personal choices.*

8. *Go for the good of the whole.*

9. *Don't knee jerk.*

10. *Ensure sustainability.*

Creative Memories' guiding principles are one of the three key components of our corporate culture (along with our mission and values shown in the front of the book). The guiding principles were first documented in March 1994 to guide our decision making and to help drive decision making down into all levels of our employee-owner base. At the time, we had about 3,500 consultants and under $10 million in annual sales.

The guiding principles evolved, as we did, and to adapt to our needs they underwent substantial rewriting in 1998 and 2002 as well as ever-changing interpretation and application. They will continue to evolve out of necessity.

Why do we have guiding principles? They help us make sound, consistent business decisions.

Ronald Bernbeim, a researcher on global business ethics, validated the importance of having principles in an organization in his speech (2002), "Wittgenstein's Bedrock: What Business Ethicists Do." He said, ". . . sustainable development and citizenship—worthy objectives in their own way—have little meaning in the absence of organizational commitment to principled business decision making."

He supported this point by focusing on Enron's "sustainable development" initiatives and "public spiritedness." Although the company was widely recognized for finding alternative energy sources and investing in their communities, when corporate scandal became public in the early part of this century, Enron's positive activities were viewed as a façade to hide corruption.

While we do not anticipate the need to ward off corruption in our organization, knowing that we have a common vision and purpose—as directed by our guiding principles—provides checks and balances that allow for consistent, appropriate decision making.

In our earliest days of the business, we all had core job responsibilities and we were also responsible for "other duties as assigned"; however, the other duties as assigned element crept up more often than not as we worked together to get anything and everything accomplished. Every one of us would take phone orders and process sales, recruiting numbers, and consultant commissions by hand. We'd pack boxes if need be. We were only an office of 10, but we were a force.

As Creative Memories' field of independent sales contractors grew from our first 6 consultants to 64 and then to 80,000 and beyond, we had to evolve. We had to increase capacity in manufacturing, staffing, and distribution. We had to increase product development and communication lead times to accommodate the growing number of consultants and customers. For example, the time to write, print, and mail written correspondence went from 2 days to 2 weeks.

We implemented processes that integrated our growing number of departments as well as our four new manufacturing facilities.

And, for many of us, we had to learn to let go. We had spent so much time doing everything that needed to be done. As we grew, we had to match skills to new jobs and give up some of our previous responsibilities to newcomers in the organization.

We also had to stop relying on the "way it has always been done." All staff had to welcome new ideas and initiatives from "outsiders" in order to learn, grow, and succeed. In essence, we had to think and act like a larger corporation rather than a small start-up.

And, we had to stop referring to ourselves as a start-up as justification for complacency or poor service. Senior Executive Director Vicki Morgan, who was our second consultant, remembers when we communicated this to our independent sales force, "It was our fifth or sixth year in business, and Cheryl came on stage at national convention," Vicki remembers. "Cheryl said, 'We are no longer going to talk about or characterize ourselves as new or emerging. We are an established company of excellence.' We were using the word 'new' as an excuse for issues and problems. The reality is we grew so fast and needed to catch up."

We had transformed from an entrepreneurial organization to an established organization. That meant we needed different modes of operation and evaluating ourselves.

To this day, even though we are not experiencing the explosive growth of the 1990s, we are continually evaluating and improving our product, program, incentives, training, fulfillment, and all other aspects of our business. Double-digit growth in an organization with sales in the hundreds of millions can still take a toll on an organization if it doesn't look for ways to continually get better.

Whenever we set about to make change in our early days, we found ourselves having the same conversations about how to implement the change, how to communicate the change to our staff and consultants, how to support and maintain it, and so on. Finally, we decided, we needed to write these conversations down, so we could refer back to them.

We documented the conversations to help people avoid what we called "Dairy Queening." This phrase was coined by our first employee, Susan Iida-Pederson. Susan had a boyfriend in high school who had difficulty applying knowledge to different situations. For example, every Friday night, they would go on a date. That date would consist of going to the same restaurant to eat the same food with the same people.

Susan mentioned once that she would like to try something different. So they went to the Dairy Queen. And they continued to go to the Dairy Queen every Friday night to eat the same thing with the same people until she brought up that she would like to try something new. It's not that she didn't like Dairy Queen. She loved it, as most of us do. She just wanted to go there once in a while. There was so much more to explore.

Her intent was to gently let him know that she liked variety, and that they could try new things each week, maybe a movie or miniature golf. However, he could only apply her request as far as the next date. Thus, they continued to have the same conversation over and over again because he was not able to learn the lesson from just one discussion.

We found ourselves in that rut, as well. Hence, when we had conversations about implementing change, we would come back to the same discussions week after week after week. We had moved from the hamburger stand to the Dairy Queen and weren't applying our previous discussions and the lessons learned to new issues.

We documented the guiding principles—these lessons we had learned—in March 1994 so that we had a frame of reference to always keep in mind during discussions. The original incarnation was almost eight pages long. The original guiding principles included rephrasing of the original principle to clarify it as well as many examples of situations to which a principle would apply.

While the length of the original guiding principles may seem like overkill, they were essential to an explosive direct-selling start-up. In 2002, our guiding principles were streamlined to 10 succinct principles that could be easily shared and remembered.

To underscore the importance of our guiding principles, we first need to explain some important information about our program and our industry.

WHAT WE DO

As a direct-selling company, we offer products and services away from a fixed retail setting. That is, Creative Memories has tens of thousands of independent consultants who teach people how to preserve their memories safely and meaningfully; they do this by going into people's homes and teaching Home Classes instead of having people come to a retail store. Through the Home Class, consultants explain the benefits of preserving our heritage, the importance of using products tested for long-term photo storage, and the tips and tricks for getting started and maintaining the album-making tradition.

We do not have a retail storefront. Instead, our consultants are independent business owners. Metaphorically, *they* are storefronts to their customer base. In the direct-selling industry, our program is known as "party plan." We meet with a group of six to eight people in a Home Class rather than offering one-to-one sales. Our Home Classes and workshops (which provide designated time to work on albums for 5 to 100 people) have been likened to the quilting bees of days gone by. In fact, in the October 21, 2002, issue of *Newsweek* magazine, scrapbooking was called ". . . the great trend sweeping America, the 21st century quilting bee."

While we appreciate that the media has noticed this little 1.5 billion dollar scrapbooking retail industry (and our growing direct-selling venture which plans to post sales of half-a-billion dollars in 2005), we continue to be amazed when people characterize us as a trend, craft, or hobby.

Creative Memories recognizes that scrapbooking is considered the third largest craft or hobby behind cross-stitching and home-décor painting according to the Hobby Industry Association. And, that is largely because albums and album-making supplies are purchased at craft and hobby stores in the retail sector. But, to label memory preservation—which is the true focus of scrapbooking—as a passing fancy or something people do for fun in their spare time truly diminishes the value and importance of creating keepsake albums.

Time magazine had this to say about scrapbooking in 2000:

*You can't take back the high-cut bikini you
wore at the company retreat . . . or the blond
hair extensions that seemed so natural at the time . . .
but you can select the photograph that conveniently
cuts off your thighs.*

*That's just what folks across the country are doing:
convening to cut and snip at their histories; to turn
inconvenient realities into Kodak moments; to prove,
in other words, that the past is perfectible. They meet
to make scrapbooks.*

This is a common perception of scrapbooking in the media and in the general public. The attention is paid to the unique stories, those stories of people who make a hot-pink album devoted to their Barbie collection or those who spend 4 hours on an album page that includes pop-up and peek-a-boo elements and only one photograph. (Don't know those phrases? Don't worry. You don't need to in order to create a lasting legacy.) We recognize, embrace, and respect that everyone will have their own personal album-making themes and album style. That is, after all, one of the beauties of album making. They help define who we are. But, in general, album making is not merely about a craft or hobby. It is not about being creative. And it is not about spending hours and hours to complete a page.

At Creative Memories we are about traditions, legacies, and passing on our heritage—about celebrating the extraordinary moments of everyday life. We are also about helping people complete their album projects. And, let's be honest, with so many things competing for our time, the last thing anybody wants to do is spend hours wading through their backlog of pictures. We understand that and have chosen to be there every step of the way to help people. And, through our Home Classes and workshops, we offer a nurturing environment for people to work on album projects with friends, family, and other album-making enthusiasts.

This, in essence, is our mission. And our mission is what draws most of our consultants to Creative Memories. Our consultants want to help others create legacies.

Other reasons consultants choose to join Creative Memories include

- Being able to spend time in a fun, social setting with others.
- The opportunity to earn extra income.
- Business ownership that is flexible enough for family to come first.

Our consultants look to us for rewarding work, flexibility, income, and a social outlet. We look to them for belief in our mission and a desire to share that mission and Creative Memories' opportunities with others.

Creative Memories is one of more than 150 companies that are members of the Direct Selling Association. And, regardless of why people choose to start a home-based business, one thing remains constant. Our sales force is made up of independent contractors who don't necessarily need us. A direct-selling opportunity is not usually their family's primary source of income. In other words, they are a volunteer sales force.

Some join direct selling because they want the social interaction that comes with home parties. Some may have a limited financial need—like wanting extra spending money or finances for private schooling. All of our consultants believe deeply in Creative Memories' mission. Nonetheless, they are volunteers. And it is our obligation to ensure that we make business decisions that are in their best interest as well as in the best interests of the company and our customers in order to keep them. These are not mutually exclusive. We must act in the best interest of all three groups.

Thus, Creative Memories' guiding principles became the grid that we lay over all business decisions. Since 1994, they have guided us to help make sound decisions that benefit all three groups, and they will continue to guide us for decades to come.

THE IMPORTANCE OF FLEXIBILITY

Although the guiding principles have been around since 1994, that doesn't mean they do not change and evolve. In fact, we welcome our employee-owners to challenge the principles, to test them, to define how they apply to current times.

Our guiding principle "Make it easy" is the perfect example of how an application may change over time. In our early days of operation, it was common for consultants to wait on hold for 45 minutes or more to place an order. This wait usually occurred at the beginning of the month (when new products were introduced and everyone had to have them) or at the end of the month (when everyone who had waited to place their minimum order requirement decided it was time to do so).

In the early days, Make it easy meant that we would help consultants with every aspect of their order while they were on the phone. We would help them track and tally their order and calculate taxes. The calls took 15 to 20 minutes each. Sometimes they would take longer as we asked how their families were doing.

While this worked when we had a few hundred consultants, the same practices would have devastating effects when we had thousands of consultants. Thus, Make it easy evolved to providing more ordering options for consultants (including fax, mail, and Internet ordering) as well as ordering tools that help consultants track inventory and calculate taxes and shipping charges automatically.

In 2001, our new Chief Operating Officer, Asha Morgan Moran, joined us. And, as she learned the Creative Memories' culture and acclimated, she questioned the principles and their continued relevance to our organization.

Creative Memories had just been through a structural reorganization. Our executive management team and functional areas within sales, marketing, and shared services were realigned. Our staff had new job responsibilities, work teams, and leadership. Asha felt it was the ideal time to reevaluate the guiding principles, refresh them, and share them with employee-owners. "We had experienced several personnel changes. People took on new job responsibilities and others joined the organization," Asha said. "It was appropriate for us to establish a new baseline to work from. The guiding principles allowed us to do that."

While she and a team of employee-owners were able to streamline the original language (eight pages worth) to the concise group of 10 guiding principles we have today, what she found was that the guiding principles still held true after so many years, although their applications may have changed.

PASSING GUIDING PRINCIPLES ON

Having guiding principles articulated and documented is not enough for them to have an impact on an organization. That would simply be paying lip service to them. The guiding principles, in order to be effective, must be visible in the organization, shared with all employees, and continually reinforced. Why? In our case, for example, more than 69 percent of our staff has been with us 5 years or less. That's a lot of newcomers to the organization.

Some of them bring new expertise to the table. Others help manage the workload. All are employee-owners and must do their best to ensure the sustainability of the organization.

Teaching all employees Creative Memories' guiding principles ensures that they understand the relationship between Creative Memories, its employee-owners, consultants, customers, and the direct-selling and retail industries. Teaching the guiding principles also ensures employee-owners know why we make the decisions we do. This, in turn, has helped us drive decision making down to managers and department staff.

Before we ramped up our operations and staffing to support exciting—and turbulent—growth, we used to invite our employee-owners to attend our weekly management meetings. The purpose was twofold: we wanted them to overhear our strategic plans and business discussions, and we hoped they would learn and retain what drives our decision making, so they could apply what they learned to their jobs.

As Rhonda recalls, "We wanted to be able to train employees to make decisions on their own. But, as we grew, our management meetings became standing room only. We needed to find a way—a concise guidebook—to help our new employees make the right decisions for our organization."

The guiding principles became our training manual and reference book for new and existing employee-owners to understand why we make the decisions we do.

Today, all new employee-owners receive a copy of the guiding principles to hang at their workstation to guide them in their planning, implementation, and decision making.

Whenever we launch a new international market, our international staff is routinely trained on the guiding principles and how they relate to our business decisions and day-to-day operations. They join us with years of experience in direct selling, but they do not know our corporate culture. Therefore, any new international management hires are brought to the home office in St. Cloud, Minnesota, where they hear about our principles. Ongoing presentations and correspondence always includes the principles that apply to the subject at hand. And the international employees are asked to operate their market on the same principles, so we ensure that they are operating the business in a consistent way. For example, as they develop their program and incentives, they will be reminded of the principle "Operate from least to most." As they examine promotional opportunities to build their market, they will be reminded of the principle "Protect the relationship." Every interaction and activity is tied to a principle.

We also refer to the guiding principles frequently when communicating with our consultants. The principles are mentioned in phone conversations, stage presentations, written articles, and more. We want our field to be comfortable with and understand how we operate. While consultants may not agree with every decision we make, they do have a comfort level knowing we have established, longstanding principles to guide our discussions. For example, we occasionally hear from consultants who want to know why we do not offer cars or mortgage subsidies as part of our compensation plan for them. Their argument is that other direct-selling companies have similar incentives, and we should be more like the other companies.

At Creative Memories, one of our guiding principles is that we respect personal choices; we do not dictate lifestyles. So, our compensation will provide the income for consultants to purchase cars or bigger houses, if that is what they choose. We will not impose that lifestyle choice on them. We don't want to ever be put in a position to have to take something away from a consultant or have them publicly embarrassed if they lose their house or car. Consultants may not be happy with this decision; however, they know why we have made the decision.

Finally, we share our guiding principles at our home office. All of our conference rooms have the guiding principles framed on the wall, so employee-owners can refer to them as they collaborate on projects.

One of the most rewarding times for me is when I'm in a meeting or listening to a team working on a project, and the guiding principles are brought up as a natural part of our language, a natural part of operating our business. These times only reinforce the value, timelessness, and necessity of Creative Memories' guiding principles in our day-to-day operations. These times also reinforce how deeply ingrained they are in our culture.

If your organization does not have documented core principles to guide decision making, I strongly recommend establishing a committee to define and draft them. Guiding principles allow organizations to have a consistent framework for doing business, a clear point of reference to drive decision making into the ranks of employees, and an objective method for communicating how and why decisions are made.

The next 10 chapters each focus on one of the guiding principles. We'll discuss the historical significance of each principle as well as how it applies today to different aspects of Creative Memories and how it can be applied to you and your company.

CHAPTER 4

OPERATE FROM LEAST TO MOST

❧———————❧

*As we increase performance criteria, the role of
technology in our business, awards, and program options,
we are responsible for taking incremental steps and not
fostering an environment where we cannot live up to
precedents we have set or cannot outdo ourselves.*

Our first guiding principle is Operate from least to most.

What does this principle mean? It means that as Creative Memories implements change in our product, program, and corporation—whether it be a new performance measurement or the use of technology—we are responsible for taking incremental steps. In other words, we don't have to do everything all at once. Instead, we must implement change in steps, measure results, adjust accordingly, and act again.

This principle also means that we cannot foster an environment where we cannot live up to precedents that we have set or where we cannot outdo ourselves.

Finally, the principle means we do not implement too many changes at any one given time, so we don't overwhelm our consultants, our customers, and ourselves.

TECH TALK: HOW MUCH IS TOO MUCH?

The most obvious business application for the principle Operate from least to most is in the technology area. With daily introductions, upgrades, and innovations, it is easy to become overwhelmed, over-automated, and overbudget. Therefore, we've taken our techno steps one at a time.

In 1996 when the World Wide Web was really becoming a resource for communication and research for the average person, Creative Memories determined it was the appropriate time for us to explore our use of it. And, based on our principle of Operate from least to most, we determined that our first step should be simply having a Web presence so we could be found by anybody who was searching for companies that offered photo-safe albums, album-making supplies, or a rewarding career opportunity.

As a direct-selling company, our best form of advertising and lead generation is the word-of-mouth advertising that our customers do. When a customer has a positive experience with his or her consultant at a Home Class or workshop, that positive experience is relayed over and over again. Our customers share their favorite family or vacation albums, or they talk with friends and family about how working on an album helped them cope with a difficult time in their life. They also share stories about how their Creative Memories' consultant helped them every step of the way with supplies, guidance, and encouragement. With that type of endorsement, we didn't really need the Web. Our company was doubling in size every 3 years without it. We simply grew the old-fashioned way.

In 1998, we decided to take the next step and implemented an online ordering system for our consultants (lead generation was still not a necessary use of the Web for us). Even though we had done our homework and were able to document that more than 90 percent of our consultant base owned and used a computer, the implementation yielded interesting results. Very few people used it.

While our demographics supported the implementation, our psy-chographics (how our consultants felt about using computers and how computers were integrated into their daily lifestyle) didn't support it. And, at the time, very few of them logged on to place orders. Although an online ordering system was a time-saving tool for consultants, they didn't have a comfort level navigating the ordering site. And they didn't necessarily trust their confidential information being sent over the World Wide Web.

This, in turn, lead to our next step in implementing technology: training in how to use it. As a result, every regional and national convention we held included training on using the Internet as a business tool. Our magazines included training articles on how to quickly and easily place orders on the Internet. Our preprinted stationery promoted using the online ordering system. And, in every correspondence, we promoted the safety features built into our system, so consultants would trust placing their orders online.

Many years later, the popularity and comfort level of online ordering has increased dramatically, and by 2003 more than 70 percent of monthly incoming orders from our field are via the Internet.

Since then, we have developed a complete Web business. Our consultant site, CMC-Network, has grown to serve as the main vehicle for communication, ordering, and education. It is our quickest, most reliable means of communicating with our field.

However, it has not replaced paper. That just doesn't fit who we are, and we are okay with that. We still mail consultants their business activity reports, monthly magazines, promotional pieces, and business correspondence. Although these things are available online, our consultants love holding actual documents in their hands.

Our next step was to update our static public site to include hundreds of dynamic pages that are updated daily, weekly, monthly, and quarterly, so customers and passersby can be inspired and educated to work on their album projects. The public site originally only contained one page devoted to our history, one page about our product, one page about being a consultant, one page about being a hostess, and one page with contact information.

The new site, launched 4 years later in September 2000, includes an Idea Center, where customers can be inspired with new page layout ideas and quotes of the day. It also includes the Tech Center where our scientists share information about long-term photo storage, digital imaging, and the history and longevity of photographic prints. The What's New section promotes new product. And,we offer a complete online catalog of The Creative Memories Collection. We also ask for personal album-making testimonials in the Share Our Stories section, and we go into greater detail about Creative Memories' opportunities for consultants, hostesses, and customers.

And, finally, we implemented online tools that allow our consultants to better serve their existing customer base. Consultants now have a means to post their Home Class and workshop schedule, to share new product information, and to take residual sales orders from existing customers.

Customers also have the ability to surf the Web site at creativememories.com to find a consultant near them. By clicking on our consultant locator button, customers can enter their zip code and find the contact information for a consultant who lives in or near the same zip code. One fact remains, though. The Internet's main purpose in our business is not lead generation and new business. The Internet is simply another tool to conduct business with current customers. Direct selling is a people business. We develop relationships with our customers through one-on-one interaction and gatherings. The Internet will not replace that. It only reinforces and serves as an additional means of communicating, connecting, and serving others.

Although our consultants have grown increasingly comfortable with online business tools, this does not mean that we have a blanket invitation to pursue technology with reckless abandon. We must safeguard cost containment, quality, functionality, and ease of use. And any implementation must include rigorous training and technical support.

Now, we need to address the second part of this principle: not setting a precedence that we cannot live up to.

In January 2000, we introduced an Internet service provider (ISP) that was customized for our consultants' business and family needs. We launched the service at 22 regional conventions to approximately 10,000 of our consultants, and we provided technical support through an outside service provider.

Thousands of consultants immediately signed up for the ISP; however, insufficient installation instructions and poor technical support quickly ended the program's credibility. It was eventually discontinued, and we had a public relations project on our hands to reestablish *our* credibility with consultants.

Our lesson here, for the principle Operate from least to most, was not that the technology was too advanced or complicated for our consultants. Our lesson was that our launches also had to be implemented in steps, from least to most, so we could manage our service levels and provide our consultants the opportunity to integrate technology without being overwhelmed. By 2000, we had built a strong following for any technological tools we introduced. As a result of that following, the initial response toward the ISP was overwhelming, and we simply could not support the volume of consultants signing up. We also could not live up to the service levels our consultants were accustomed to when contacting technical support for installation and troubleshooting questions.

Since then, we have adjusted our program launch plan to follow the Operate from least to most principle in terms of setting precedence. With any major launch of technology or service, we introduce it to our leadership first. That way, we have a limited number of individuals using the program or service. We can implement, measure, and adjust accordingly. Then, we launch to a larger, but manageable, group of consultants. This could be anyone who attends a particular event, a particular geographic region, or any other predetermined category. Once this second phase of a launch is complete, we will open up a general launch to the entire consultant base.

By operating from least to most on a service or technology launch, we are able to manage our service levels and maintain a positive, credible image with our consultants.

THE CHALLENGE OF CHOICE IN SKU PROLIFERATION

Operating from least to most also impacts our product line.

Within the Creative Memories Collection, we have everything novice and expert album makers need to preserve their heritage in keepsake photo albums. Consultants offer their customers the finest albums, papers, stickers, die-cut shapes, cutting tools, adhesives, writing tools, and step-by-step idea books. Creative Memories even has the Memory Mate organizational system to carry and store albums and supplies.

Scrapbooking stores and scrapbooking magazines continue to pop up everywhere. Craft trends come and go. And we know with these come the endless barrage of decorative enhancements for albums. Grommets, wire, paint, stamps, pop-up pages, peek-a-boo pages, and "heavy metal" have all taken center stage in the craft and hobby markets. We continually hear from our field and our consumers via our product suggestion form, e-mails, and one-on-one conversation that we need to keep up with these latest trends and offerings. In fact, we receive around 50,000 official suggestions each year. That's a lot of product requests.

We get requests for every possible sticker, every possible paper color or design, every possible wire, grommet, punch, and stamp that is available in the retail market for album making—and for some that aren't. For example, many people have suggested that we need breastfeeding stickers since over 98 percent of our consumers are women and feeding newborns is an important, memorable part of being a parent. While the brainstorming session to determine those sticker icons would be quite entertaining, we're quite certain we will not be offering those in our line any time soon. And, to be honest, we will never have every product to satisfy every whim of every consumer. That is not who we are, and we communicate that often.

We are about simple pages and completed albums. We are about getting stories told through meaningful journaling. We are about capturing how we live, whom we love, and what we value.

So, in keeping with the principle of operating from least to most, we decided to only introduce a few new decorative accessories and idea books to keep our line fresh and exciting for consultants and consumers, but we will never be the be-all and end-all of decorative supplies. It's just not possible. Instead, our focus on photo-safe supplies and speed tools allows consumers to get their album projects completed safely and easily.

In a recent study we conducted, we learned that 55 percent of those who do not preserve memories in keepsake albums believe album making is time consuming and too crafty. Whenever we run into people who do not work on their albums, we usually hear that they believe it takes 1 to 2 hours to complete one double-page spread in an album. This perception of album making is a result of scrapbooking stores and scrapbooking magazines featuring and promoting decorative pages that are awash with papers, paints, and pop-up and peek-a-boo elements. These pages might even have only one picture on them.

Our focus on simple pages and completed albums allows us to reach out to those who have backlogs of photographs, memorabilia, and stories to be captured on album pages. We encourage others to include a minimum of four pictures per page. And, if journaling isn't included, the album isn't complete. They say a picture is worth a thousand words. If those words aren't captured for future generations, the picture isn't worth the paper it is printed on.

Fifty years from now, our families will not be captivated by the stickers and papers that we placed on an album page. They will be enthralled by the written word.

Operating from least to most keeps us focused on our mission of helping people capture their special stories in safe, meaningful keepsake albums.

WHERE TO START

Operating from least to most is valuable at all phases of a business's life cycle.

During start-up, many entrepreneurs become consumed with looking like a business. They invest their time and money in purchasing leather office chairs and equipment, designing a logo, and setting up a storefront with a neon sign.

The reality is, if you have a product or service that you are ready to share and you have a means of getting it to your customers, your essential start-up items are business cards (so people can keep in contact with you), a promotional flyer or catalog detailing your product or service (it can be one-color instead of four-color with high gloss—remember, least to most), and a means to interact with consumers (try starting in your home before you venture out to rent space). While computers are nice to have, initial handwritten ledgers, high-lighters, and stick-on notes do the trick. Start slow. Build as you go. Spend your time on the key business building activities, like providing quality product and service, prospecting, and follow-up.

Through the high-growth phase of a business, the initial reaction is to hire, hire, hire. Unfortunately, there may come a time when one has to fire, fire, fire. And, nobody wants to do that.

At our company, especially during the mid-1990s, we were routinely told by staff that we didn't hire fast enough, that we were slow to get things done. In reality, we were operating from least to most. We knew we were in a crunch but didn't want to overcommit ourselves to staff that we may one day have to let go. Instead, we looked at outsourcing options, realigning job descriptions, and bringing in outside people on a contract basis. It's not that we didn't want to hire. We didn't want to overhire and inflate our overhead. We just wanted to be sure we weren't reacting to a short-term burst of activity.

When businesses mature and are looking for ways to breathe new life into their organizations, the principle of Operating from least to most is essential to the bottom line. The tendency for some is to spend millions in advertising dollars to attract new consumers and build brand awareness. But, I've read quite often that it takes 80 percent more time and money to attract new customers than it does to make the ones you have happy. So, why not reinvest in energizing your current customers?

When The Antioch Company moved me out to St. Cloud, Minnesota, to oversee the buyout of the then-bankrupt Holes-Webway Company in 1986, we had a strong, steady base of loyal consumers that kept our company going. While the big accounts were nice to land, the investment and reliance on them can have devastating effects. If one big account chose to no longer need our products, we would have been hit hard. We preferred to have several small steady customers who consistently accounted for 50 percent of our product orders than one large one who accounted for 80 percent.

Operating from least to most is beneficial for all phases of a business's life cycle. This principle will help determine where financial and human resources are best allocated. This principle will allow an organization to have a vision for the future and to create a step-by-step action plan to reach that vision. And operating from least to most will protect an organization from setting hiring, performance, and service standards that it cannot live up to.

AND WHAT ABOUT THE FROUFROU?

In the direct-selling industry, about 75 percent of our job as a leader is to recognize and celebrate our independent sales force for their consistency, commitment, and achievement. This can take the form of printed recognition, on-stage recognition, tangible awards like jewelry, special event attendance, and financial gain. While recognition is a standard part of business in the direct-selling industry, recognition is something that all organizations can benefit from. Everyone enjoys accolades for a job well done or knowing that they are appreciated for the work they do.

A natural human tendency when planning awards and celebrations is to make it big. And while this may be fun to plan, it does come with an expense and with an expectation. Operating from least to most provides us with the opportunity to analyze where we will get the biggest return on our investment. At some point, the quality of the experience does not necessarily justify the cost.

The best analogy I can use to describe this is like buying a new suit. The difference between buying a $50 suit and a $500 suit is obvious. The richness of the fabric, the conciseness of the cut and fit, and the attention to detail will be clear in the more expensive suit. People will notice.

The difference between a $500 suit and a $5,000 suit may not be as obvious. The fabric may be imported, the suit may be hand-stitched, and the tag may promote a well-known suit manufacturer.

However, these things are not evident to the casual observer. The wearer will know about them and feel good about them. The observer will not. So what was gained?

When planning incentives and recognition, it's important to recognize where the distinction comes in.

When recognizing someone in print, the mileage of a name in 7-point type on page 32 of a black-and-white newsletter does go a long way. People will search for their name. They will highlight it, and they will show it to other people. They will be proud. If this is where you need to start, it is okay. You can always improve from there, and operating from least to most gives you that option.

If planning a formal banquet, for example, do you want to invest in the food and a gift for all attendees to take home, or do you want the $3,000 swan ice sculpture that drips pink champagne from its mouth? People will be impressed by the ice sculpture, but what is the take-away value?

At Creative Memories, we do offer incentives, such as jewelry and trips, to consultants who reach predetermined sales and recruiting goals. But one of the most rewarding forms of recognition that we hear about quite often didn't cost us a thing.

We have an annual event at our home office for field members who have been promoted to our director level. It is called New Directors Training. A few years ago, on a whim, someone suggested we should have employees waiting out front of the building when the coach pulled up to the curb with our 50 new directors. So we did.

As the new directors stepped off the bus and walked to the building, they walked through a receiving line of employees who were applauding them, congratulating them, and welcoming them to our office. People cried. People took pictures. And, every year now, we hear that that was a moment when they felt so appreciated and so proud to be a part of the Creative Memories team. Small gestures like that go a long way.

Lee Morgan, our CEO, consistently reminds us that this type of personal, inexpensive recognition and celebration has lasting effects. He recalls:

When Cheryl first moved to St. Cloud to oversee the buyout of Webway, she was building relationships with bankers, lawyers, the employees, and the sales reps. Everybody was suspicious of us for buying the bankrupt photo-album manufacturer. They thought we were really sneaky or really stupid.

Cheryl helped put an end to all that. She would meet with everybody one-on-one or in groups and make them feel good about our organization. And, she did it through unconventional means. Her first winter in Minnesota was a particularly harsh one. You have to remember that she had spent her entire life living within one hour of where she was born. After her divorce, she packed up and headed north where she was greeted by 8-foot snow drifts and a lot of cold. She used that to our company's advantage.

One winter, she invited our retail sales reps to St. Cloud for a sales meeting, and she made the event a Hawaiian theme. The first evening was a celebration, and everyone enjoyed it. The sales reps had the opportunity to network in a casual atmosphere and to unwind. That set the stage for the business meeting the next day. Everyone was relaxed and comfortable starting business because they felt appreciated.

Cheryl was also known for jotting notes on commission checks and other business correspondence. The notes would simply say "Thank you for all you do"or "Look forward to seeing you soon." This got through to people. And, you have to remember that most of these folks were old, hard-nosed and jaded business people. Cheryl helped break that down through simple, consistent recognition.

When I hear these stories and know people remember simple, thoughtful gestures, it continually validates one thing: coworkers, vendors, and consumers all love to be recognized and feel appreciated, regardless of age, status, or achievement. They are positively affected by random acts of kindness and gratitude. These acts can be simple and inexpensive. And of all investments a business can make, they can have the most impact.

Notes of encouragement, a stroll through the hallway to say hello to everyone, a few minutes of your time to ask how someone is doing— it all goes a long way. And it is the least you can do in your quest to make people feel the most appreciated and valued in your organization.

BUT ALWAYS DO YOUR BEST WORK

Operating from least to most helps cast a vision of where an organization can be. It helps establish incremental steps to reach that vision. It can help define where the biggest impact will be. And it allows organizations to continually implement change, analyze the effects of that change, and act accordingly.

One thing I want to make clear regarding the principle Operate from least to most is that it does not mean we do not do something well. Operate from least to most does not equal mediocrity. If, for example, you want to implement a significant change to your product line (like adding a new product category or eliminating a product category), you can't invest all of your financial and human resources in updating operations and neglect to include the customer communication piece. In the last few years, a local company that provides compliance software to banks determined it was going to eliminate the DOS-side of its software programs and technical support. For legitimate financial reasons, it made sense to focus on the Windows-based platform. Now, this company could easily have taken the path of least resistance by simply eliminating the DOS software and support. This approach carries with it the attitude that the DOS-based customers simply needed to "get with the program" and "move into the new millennium" as far as technology goes.

Fortunately, the company realized the importance of helping their DOS customers transition comfortably from their old system to the new. So the company invested in monthly communications to their DOS customers—through letters, faxes, or promotional flyers—during a 2-year transition period. The company's ultimate goal was to preserve the relationship it had built with these customers by helping them upgrade technology and move to an easier system. The company didn't want to "cut the cord," so to speak. The company wanted to ensure a lifelong relationship with the banks.

In another example, if you can only afford to produce a black-and-white photocopied newsletter your first years in business, make it look good. Don't assume that because it is not four-color, high-gloss magazine paper that it can't look polished and professional. The image conveys a message as much as the content of it.

Operating from least to most also does not serve as an excuse to be complacent. Too many people hang their hat on the status quo. They believe the way things have always been done is the way to continue doing them. We have to be open to new ideas and recognize that what was acceptable 10 years ago (heck, with technology advancing at the rate it is, even 3 months ago) may not be a realistic expectation today.

We need to continually move forward with ideas to improve our product, program, and people—both internal staff and external sales force and vendors. And we have to understand that not everything can be done at once. Our challenge, then, is to identify who and what we want to be and move in that direction step by step.

As our COO Asha Moran says, "We can't always wait for things to be perfect. We should understand and see our vision for what 100 percent looks like and take the steps to get there. That vision of 100 percent drives the incremental change."

FIGHT THE FIRE IN FRONT OF YOU

Over the years, Creative Memories' growth was overwhelming at times. Often, those of us on staff would pass each other in the hallways with a weary look in our eyes. Yet we would go to our desks and tackle our next item on the to-do list. Little by little, we came out ahead.

In all stages of business and life, people can feel overwhelmed by all that they have to do and all that they want to do. The best way to get through that feeling and start accomplishing tasks is to simply slow down, make a list of what is important, and get to work. Don't think about everything. Fight the fire in front of you. This is also operating from least to most. Rather than trying to do everything at once or the most that you can do, manage your tasks in smaller pieces. By conquering one or two tasks at a time, you will feel less overwhelmed and more accomplished.

I often say we are either moving forward and growing or standing still and dying. We can drive our business performance by going in the direction of our vision. Operating from least to most allows us to move forward at a steady, well-thought-out pace.

CHAPTER 5

EMBRACE THE ABUNDANCE MENTALITY

*We are responsible for being aware of our relationship
to the scrapbooking and direct-selling industries and embracing
competition as a good and necessary part of growth.*

In the book *Hard to Get*, Diana Vreeland—the extravagant, long-time columnist for *Harper's Bazaar*—is quoted as saying, "Never compete. Never. Watching the other guy is what kills all forms of energy." We tend to agree, only we phrase it differently in our second guiding principle, Embrace the abundance mentality.

We have competition. And, like most organizations, we have it on multiple fronts. We all have competition for time, money, energy, space. At Creative Memories, our own industries (scrapbooking and direct selling) provide competition as well.

Creative Memories is aware of its relationship to the scrapbooking industry and the direct-selling industry. We are aware of this competition, and we embrace it as a necessary and positive part of doing business. This competition simply raises awareness about what we do and allows us to define and position ourselves to our needs and our consumers' expectations. We don't compete. We sell to our strengths. We believe in who we are. And, we know there is plenty for everyone.

ON THE STORE FRONT

According to the Hobby Industry Association, in 2003, the scrapbooking segment of the craft industry was estimated to be a multibillion dollar industry, made up of a few thousand mom-and-pop retail stores and a couple of big chains.

Most of these scrapbooking shops popped up in the late 1990s and the early part of this century. We know scrapbooking magazines began appearing in the late 1990s, and now these magazines offer hundreds of products from other vendors to avid album-making enthusiasts and newcomers.

Prior to the founding of Creative Memories in 1987, very few people knew the importance of preserving memories in albums that do not chemically destroy their photographs and memorabilia. Magnetic albums, which could permanently damage photographs, dominated the market. Very few people knew the value of documenting the extraordinary moments of everyday life in keepsake albums. And nobody knew you could have a rewarding career teaching people the importance of and how-to's for memory preservation.

In 1996, when our sales force had reached 22,000 and our annual sales were over $70 million, the retail sector noticed that people were investing a lot of money in albums and album-making supplies. Retail shops began to ramp up their scrapbooking offerings by expanding their bottom-shelf placement to an entire row of stickers, pens, adhesives, decorative papers, and albums. General public awareness continued to grow.

Album and supply vendors have attempted to upgrade their products to be photo-safe like ours. Currently, though, Creative Memories is the only supplier of albums and decorative enhancements to commit to photo-safe albums and supplies. We employ a team of scientists and lab technicians in our in-house technology center to test our products for long-term storage.

And more and more people are realizing that when they print or have their pictures developed, they can't just stuff those photos away in shoeboxes and drawers and feel good about it. As the use of digital technology increases, we need to continue to reach out to those who now use a computer as the modern-day shoebox. While they have captured their memorable moments digitally, they need to commit to printing the pictures and preserving them.

Creative Memories pioneered this industry because we believed in the importance of it. We're glad that others have chosen to participate. And, through our collective efforts, we will reach millions of people throughout the world.

What competition does provide us is the opportunity to take a hard look at ourselves, our products, and our programs. Competition encourages us to define and celebrate who we are and what we stand for.

STICKING TO OUR FOCUS

Creative Memories is committed to helping others capture and preserve their special stories in safe, meaningful keepsake albums. We fulfill this by teaching people to make simple pages that document their life stories. While we do provide decorative accessories and instruction for creative pages, that is not our primary focus.

If we sell albums and supplies to people and they leave our Home Class, stuff our product high on a closet shelf and let it sit there, we have not done our job. Sure, we made the sale, but we did not fulfill our mission of preserving the past, enriching the present, and inspiring hope for the future through completed albums. This, alone, sets us apart from our retail competition. But we have so much more to offer.

Creative Memories is here for busy people. Creative Memories is here for those who simply do not know where to begin with their backlog of family photographs. Creative Memories is here for those who need the gentle encouragement and instruction for starting and maintaining the tradition of creating keepsake albums.

We know who we are. We know who we reach. And that is our focus. We do not adjust ourselves to compete with the constantly evolving retail sector. Instead, we sell to our strengths.

I know of a little shop here in town that illustrates this point. In St. Cloud, there is this small hamburger stand called Val's Rapid Service that opened as a family business in 1959. It was the first fast-food restaurant in St. Cloud. It consists of a small building with a 6 × 20 ordering area. No booths, no chairs, no fancy neon lights.

And, over the last 50 years, the city of St. Cloud has built up around it. In fact, you'd drive right by it even if you were looking for it.

The parking lot has six parking spaces (none of them big enough for an SUV). And, within 2 miles of Val's you have the modern conveniences of every fast-food chain, complete with drive-through service, kiddie playland, and plastic toys in the happy meals.

But Val's is legendary in St. Cloud for the best burgers around. The strawberry and chocolate shakes are deliciously mammoth in size and cost less than a buck, and the 2-pound bag of fries that you get is translucent with grease before you even get out the door. It is unbelievable.

Well, in August 1999, Val's went high-tech when they installed a phone and touch-screen kiosk inside their ordering area. It made the front page of the local paper as, "Val's kiosks let callers avoid lunch lines." That is about as technical as it gets. And they love it that way. So do the locals.

Val's knows the meaning of being true to its past. Val's knows that competition abounds in the fast-food sector. Yet, Val's knows and commits to what their customers value and appreciate about them. Val's knows what technology and innovation meets their goals and still offers a value-added service. And, as McDonald's fulfills its mission of never making customers drive more than 2 miles to go to a McDonald's, Val's is unphased.

That is what customer loyalty is about. That is what brand recognition is about. And that is what embracing the abundance mentality is about.

People have their loves. As consumers, they have a love for brand, price, quality, relationship, ease of use, ease of access—you name it. As businesses, we cannot be all things to all people, so we have to identify how we fit in and whom we reach. There is plenty of playing field for everybody; we simply have to position ourselves for our target market.

In 2002 Jeep Wrangler introduced an ad campaign that demonstrates it knows its market. The Only in a Jeep series celebrated its consumers' love of the ruggedness of Jeep Wranglers.

In one spot, a woman walks through a Jeep dealership and casually throws a bucket of mud on each color of Wrangler in the parking lot. On her last throw, she looks intently at the mud-covered vehicle and nods with approval. "This is the one," she proclaims to the salesperson.

Those who drive Jeep Wranglers do not invest in them for good gas mileage, the practicality, or the cargo room. Jeep Wranglers simply don't have these things. And Jeep makes no apologies for it. Jeep Wranglers are positioned and packaged as rugged and fun. Jeep Wranglers have a romantic aura about them that is simply unmatched in other vehicles. Jeep would be foolish to go after the minivan market. The needs are different.

The minivan market wants safety for their family, plenty of seating, and sippy-cup holders for the kids. That built-in DVD player is a plus, too. The overriding benefit of the well-equipped minivan is a peaceful, organized venture for the family. And that venture can be 5 miles to the daycare or across country to camp at a national park.

When it comes to new business, rarely will we find a new idea; we simply find new packaging and positioning. Or, in our case, we perfect the highest quality standards above the competition. It all comes down to sippy-cup holders and bike racks. While it is sound business practice to have goals and reach them (e.g., capturing a certain percentage of market share, increased sales, or increased number of store fronts), this cannot be done without identifying who you are and what you provide to your largest customer base.

Since we are talking about cars, I wanted to bring up another example of a used car dealership that I was drawn to because of its advertisements. Basically, this dealership was a no-frills, no-hassle used car dealership for people who liked options presented to them straight. Its ad campaign highlighted all of this.

One ad promoted what was included as "standard features." Features included a steering wheel, four tires, and an engine that worked. A radio was a possibility, too. Another mentioned that the dealership didn't charge for fancy services and contracts, so the buyer shouldn't expect any. Another ad also boasted that the dealership offered choices: take it or leave it.

Clearly, this organization knew what spoke to its customers; it also knew what set it apart from its competition. Now, would I buy a car from this dealership? Probably not, but I have some relatives who would love to.

Competition helps us define and celebrate these differences and determine where we fit in. Competition also helps us strengthen our differences.

PARTY ON!

Several hundred thousand people join one of the more than 150 direct-selling member companies each year. And, each year, the number of companies to choose from increases as start-ups introduce their products, services, and career opportunities.

These companies offer everything. If there is a consumer need, some direct-selling venture will be able to meet it. And, in some instances, more than one company will. Look at cosmetics and skin care, for example. Long-time favorites like Avon (which began in 1886 as the California Perfume Company) and Mary Kay (which began direct selling in 1963) continue to find exciting growth and opportunity even when faced with competition from newcomers to the industry like The Body Shop at Home (introduced in 2003). Not only that, they are faced with the reality that anyone can walk into a gas station and buy a tube of lipstick and some facial moisturizer. Direct competition is high in these product categories. So why do they continue to find success? The answer is simple: brand loyalty and love of the direct-selling distribution model. Consumers love particular products. And, in the case of direct selling, consumers love the personal, one-on-one relationships they form with their independent salesperson. Consumers know their Creative Memories, Mary Kay, or Kirby vacuum cleaner sales representatives truly understand their individual wants and needs. Consumers know their direct-selling representative will offer quality product and service. And consumers know their direct-selling representative will preserve a lifelong relationship with them.

Creative Memories until recently has not been faced with any direct competition in the retail or direct-selling industries. However, indirect competition for time, money, and energy is always evident. People only have so much of these three things to invest. They will invest in what they feel is of value to them.

Creating keepsake albums is not for everyone. Direct selling is not for everyone. Anyone can do them; not everyone wants to. We offer what we have and welcome everyone to take part as a consumer, a hostess of a party, or a consultant. Some may even choose to be all three at some point.

The August 11, 2003, issue of *Fortune* magazine highlighted the direct-selling industry in a special section titled, "Corporate America's New Salesforce: Despite the sputtering economy, independent contractors are reenergizing the U.S. retail industry through direct selling."

The article focused on what the Direct Selling Association calls "cyclical immunity." In a strong economy, direct sellers do well because the buying public is investing in premium products and services that add value to their lives.

When the economy is less favorable—or the emotional state of the general public is shaken, like after the September 11 terrorist attacks—people turn to direct sellers. Under these circumstances, they are seeking comfort in what is familiar: the relationship and trust they have built with their personal distributor, the quality of products they have come to love, and the social aspect of gathering at a home party rather than venturing into public places. In other words, direct selling is relatively immune to the ebb and flow of consumer buying patterns that the retail sector must navigate. Yes, direct selling does experience peak times (like the holiday buying season) and low times (the few weeks when families are preparing their children for the start of the new school year). But, overall, the buying patterns are relatively consistent despite the state of the economy.

The career opportunity is attractive, too, as people seek out control of their own destiny. As home-based business owners in the direct-selling industry, our consultants can define and achieve their own business goals with little initial investment. And they can build their business around their personal priorities. For example, a consultant can choose to work between 8 a.m. and 3 p.m. while the kids are at school. And she even has the flexibility to take a day off each week to volunteer at school if she chooses. A consultant can choose to make a full-time career out of her business, but those 40 hours a week can be allocated when it is most appropriate for her family. She can choose to work some nights, some days, some weekends. The key is that she determines her own schedule.

Consultants will get out of their business what they put into it, be it a social outlet, additional spending money, or a full-time career. The beauty of this business, regardless of the products or services a company offers, is that it all comes down to personal choice.

After the *Fortune* article broke, a few consultants called in to Creative Memories to express their disappointment in it. Although the article provided increased awareness of our organization and the direct-selling industry as a whole, it also provided the names of many other direct-selling opportunities that, in some consultants' terms, would "steal people away from Creative Memories." This was a perfect teaching moment to explain the principle of embracing the abundance mentality. If we are true to ourselves and our mission, people will stay with us if it is the right choice for them. There is plenty for everybody.

Embracing the abundance mentality also impacts our sales force's perception of welcoming new consultants to our team. Consultants who choose to build and strengthen their home-based business know that they should recruit and build a team. Early on in consultants' careers, they may choose not to recruit because they don't want to hurt their own chances of building a customer base. They want all the potential customers in their own communities. The reality is, though, a consultant in a community of 50,000 cannot possibly provide great service to all 50,000 community members. Ten consultants in that community cannot provide great service to 10,000 community members. And, even still, 100 consultants in that community may have trouble providing great service to 500 people. Great service is the cornerstone of what we do in direct selling. It is in a consultant's best interest to build a team to help share the Creative Memories mission of preserving memories.

As I said before, there is plenty for everybody.

In a strategic planning meeting, one of our newer employee-owners questioned this guiding principle. She asked, "You mean we actually support competition?"

Our COO responded, "No. We understand competition is there. But, we do not let it paralyze us or cause us to become something we are not."

Creative Memories was the first and remains the best resource for capturing the world's autobiography one memory at a time. We are Memory Keeping at Its Best. Why? Because we help busy people with backlogs of photographs preserve their special stories in keepsake albums. We help them provide a lasting legacy for their families. We help them capture the extraordinary moments of everyday life. We help them document how they live, who they love, and what they value. This brings a sense of peace, identity, and belonging for our album makers. We stay true to that, and everything else falls into place.

Organizations need to have a commitment to enrich the lives of their consumers. How do we make life easier, more interesting, and more affordable for them? It's never about us, as a business, even though we are all guilty of thinking this way.

Think about a meeting where product development or the research and development team lead a filibuster over all the "bells and whistles" a new product has. Through "miracles" of science, technology, or innovation, the company has the ability to introduce something that revolutionizes the way people store their negatives, for example. This happened to us about 7 years ago. A team created a prototype for us of a film negative storage container that was fire-resistant and water-resistant. While it would protect a family's negatives from fire or flood, the container weighed about 40 pounds and would cost more than the average consumer was willing to spend. We know because we asked the consumers. They were not interested in a product of this kind at the price point it would be offered at. Therefore, we decided not to add it to our product line.

This incident reminds me of a scene in the movie *Jurassic Park*. Chaos theorist Dr. Ian Malcolm confronts John Hammond, the money behind the theme park to reintroduce dinosaurs to modern man. Dr. Malcolm said, ". . . your scientists were so preoccupied with whether or not they *could* that they didn't stop to think if they *should*."

Granted, the risk of introducing a 40-pound, fire-and-flood resistant box is substantially less than unleashing a genetically engineered T-rex on a theme park; nonetheless, the lesson is the same. Introducing products and services to consumers is not about us—the company—and what we *could* do. What we *could* do is more than likely not a competitive advantage. Introducing products and services that enrich consumers' lives is what we *should* do for them. Doing what we *should* is our competitive advantage.

B J. Bueno, in his *Radio Ink* column "Cult Branding," encourages an "advertising renaissance" where businesses shift their focus from the product or service to the consumer.

He writes, "True brand loyalty occurs when customers choose to love you. Make consumers the center of your marketing campaigns, because when your message connects with their hearts, their minds will follow—and soon, so will the money."

Let's consider toothpaste, for example. This is a basic household good with several brands in the marketplace. Brand awareness aside, let's look at what toothpaste provides for the consumer.

For parents of toddlers, toothpaste helps their young children grow strong, healthy teeth and hopefully prevents cavities.

For teenagers, perhaps, toothpaste provides the comfort of minty, fresh breath for the close proximity of the classroom. Teenagers have plenty of things on their minds. Bad breath should not be one of them.

For older adults, perhaps they want the comfort of having their own teeth for their lifetime rather than having to get false ones.

The same toothpaste could be available to each of these markets; however, the positioning of the toothpaste would be different.

When you think about your product or service, think about what's in it for them—the consumers. Who are we trying to reach and how will our product or service enrich their lives? The answers to these questions are what will set us apart from our competition. The answers to these questions will help us stay focused and reach out to our target market.

DON'T DOG THE OTHER GUY

Recent presidential election advertisements really reinforce the need for the guiding principle Embrace the abundance mentality. It really makes my skin crawl when I watch political advertisements. They are too busy telling me what is wrong with the other guy rather than telling me what they are going to do for us. While I recognize that only one person can be president—therefore, an abundance of the position is not readily available—selling to individual strengths would make all the candidates a winner in the long run. The general public would remember the candidates for what their strengths are and not how nasty their campaigns were. Perhaps that is what candidates—and businesses—need to focus on: the big picture win. There truly is enough opportunity for everybody. If we believe there is enough, there will be. If we think there isn't, there won't be.

I've heard often that racehorses never look to the side or behind them to see how the other horses are doing. They simply focus on the finish line and how to get across. A great day for us at Creative Memories isn't about overtaking the competition; it's really about being better than we were yesterday.

CHAPTER 6

KEEP
THE PROMISE

*We are responsible for preserving our integrity
and credibility by providing product and program
quality that meets or exceeds our promise to
Consultants, consumer and employee-owners.*

PROMISES, PROMISES, PROMISES

We make many promises in life and in business. And in both instances we must ensure that we keep them. Holding true to our word will preserve and strengthen our relationships as well as build and preserve our credibility as individuals and as businesspeople.

At Creative Memories, we are responsible for preserving our integrity and credibility by providing product and program quality that meets or exceeds our promise to consultants, consumers, and employee-owners.

What are these promises? We have several. And they all lead back to our mission statement:

We offer quality photo-safe products and information that utilizes cutting-edge technology.

We provide profitable career opportunities for those who believe in and want to share the Creative Memories' philosophy, values, and ethics.

And we offer a successful company that provides joy, dignity, and pride for Creative Memories' consultants and staff members.

For album makers everywhere, we must ensure that their special stories are safe in our albums. It's been this way since the beginning.

When Creative Memories first started in 1987, peel-and-stick page albums were popular for keeping pictures. And, while many consumers were using them to store and showcase their family stories, what they were finding was that after 10 years in those albums, the photographs would get stuck on the pages and the images were badly discolored.

No standards had been set—or at least adhered to—for safe, long-term photo storage.

Then, in the October 3, 1987, issue of the *New York Times*, this consumer concern took center stage in the article "Fading Memories: Albums Damage Photos." This piece told of how the materials and construction of many albums available at the time actually created a harsh environment for photographic prints. As James M. Reilly, director of the Image Permanence Institute at the Rochester Institute of Technology (RIT), said in the article, "An essential part of many families' heritage is in danger of being lost and few are aware of it."

Creative Memories committed at this time to ensuring that our product line continued to be the best available, beyond the quality already established through our unique binding, durability, and lifetime guarantee. Being the "best" meant being photo-safe. Our products would not accelerate the natural deterioration process of a photo, nor would they deteriorate themselves. We wanted our products to last as long as the pictures' life expectancy, if not longer.

Creative Memories' first brochure in January 1988 warned consumers of fading, discoloration, yellowing, and crumbling of photographs due to contact with bad chemicals, specifically ones with a high acid content. Damage to invaluable memories could be caused by albums, storage boxes, or the environment. This, of course, was in addition to the other aspects of our program that were promoted: the benefits of creating keepsake albums; helpful hints; page layout ideas; and advice on photo selection, journaling, and safe storage.

In other words, our promise to consultants and customers was to provide them with the best possible materials for preserving their treasured stories. We keep that promise today and have many safeguards to ensure our products will not harm precious photographs, memorabilia, and documentation.

Our in-house technology center is staffed by a passionate and intelligent team of scientists and lab technicians who rigorously test The Creative Memories Collection to ensure our product line meets or exceeds current standards for long-term photo storage. This group of employees loves their own photos and completed albums as much as they love organic chemistry and paper science. Their job is the perfect blend of both passions.

In addition to product testing, two of our scientists help define standards for long-term photo storage. Creative Memories is the only company in the scrapbook photo album industry that maintains a presence on the International Organization for Standardization's Task Group on Physical Properties and Image Permanence. The International Organization for Standardization (ISO) is responsible for standardizing everything from construction materials to child-resistant packaging. The task group establishes standards for long-term preservation of traditional and digital photographic images. Creative Memories has been a member of the committee since 1999. This relationship also helped us establish specifications for Creative Memories products that reflect current standards.

Creative Memories also provides our consultants with accurate technical information and definitions of what it means to be considered safe for long-term photo storage, so they can share this information with consumers. This is part of our promise, as well, to help our consultants feel comfortable that they have accurate and clear information to help educate others. The Creative Memories dictionary is one way that Creative Memories remains a leader. For example, in the scrapbooking industry, people refer to the term *archival* to indicate products are safe for long-term photo storage. Archival is an ambiguous term used to describe everything from backup copies of computer files to documents that will remain accessible for an indefinite time in the future. This term is no longer in use in International Standards for Imaging Materials or at Creative Memories. We do not use the term archival in Creative Memories publications or to describe Creative Memories products.

Acid-free is another unclear word. Using the descriptive acid-free is like using fat-free to describe gummy bears as a healthy snack alternative. From a scientific viewpoint acid-free is a completely meaningless word without a specific definition.

We do use the term acid-free at Creative Memories, but unlike many others in the industry, we give a specific definition of what acid-free means. Acid-free means paper material with a pH of 7.0 to 9.5, when tested using cold extraction, or adhesive material with a pH of 7.0 to 9.5, when tested using a surface probe. This definition is confusing to most nonscientists, and we don't expect our consultants to memorize it. The important thing to remember is that we have a definition. Truthfully, we don't know what most other companies mean when they use this term. As a leader in the scrapbooking industry, we can use the term acid-free with confidence, knowing that Creative Memories products are tested according to specific guidelines to be acid-free.

Creative Memories is also a leader in digital technology. We continue to emphasize the importance of printing photos either at a photo processor or at home. Photos are not preserved until they are printed and mounted in a Creative Memories album.

We have highlighted the problems with acidic ink-jet paper and with humidity-induced dye migration. Until Creative Memories published these results, the imaging industry was generally unaware of just how harmful these factors could be.

Creative Memories has also worked with the Image Permanence Institute at RIT to develop "A Consumer Guide to Traditional and Digital Print Stability." This guide is designed to help educate our consultants and customers about the best way to print and preserve digital images.

Creative Memories is the leader in providing photo-safe products and education for our consultants and consumers. Creative Memories products will continue to improve and will remain the best in the industry as we strive to meet and exceed current and future standards for long-term photo storage.

In 2001, for example, the ISO updated the standard for papers that come into contact with photographs. When we knew about this changing standard, we had to make some decisions. Do we update the product line? Do we create a product extension that meets the new standard? Or do we simply inform our consultants and consumers about the changing standards and how our products fit in?

Answering these questions involved crunching our numbers to determine increases in our SKU (Stock Keeping Unit or a numbered item that we inventory and sell) count, possible waste in our on-hand inventory, and price increases for new paper composition and milling techniques. We also couldn't overlook the cost of training to help our consultants understand and confidently explain the difference in the new standard and new paper.

Because of our third guiding principle: Keep the promise, the answers to these questions were simple. We did it all.

Creative Memories' senior paper scientist worked with our suppliers to introduce P series paper that complies with ISO 18902-2001 Standard for Photographic Enclosures. We were the first company to introduce this paper for scrapbook photo albums. It meets ISO requirements for bleed-resistance, ensuring that nothing in our keepsake albums will harm photographic memories, even in the unlikely event that albums become wet in a flood or during a fire or are exposed to high humidity conditions. Our new definition of photo-safe specifies material that complies with ISO 18902-2001 and will not accelerate the natural aging of photographs. We are the only company we know of that follows ISO guidelines and requires all photo-safe products to be bleed-resistant.

We kept our former line of papers, which met the former standard. These are now known as our D series papers. But we could no longer promote our D series paper as photo-safe because our definition of photo safety changed to reflect the latest photo safety standard. We continue to promote D series paper as acid-free, lignin-free, and buffered, and it passes the photographic activity test (part of the standard for long-term photo storage) because these terms accurately describe D series paper. However, because the D series is not bleed-resistant, we cannot call it photo-safe.

With this information, we are able to provide researched information and training to our consultants, so they can help their customers make informed decisions about memory preservation and storage. People trust us with their cherished family photographs and stories. We must never break that trust. We must never break that promise.

Now, here is the caveat. When we introduced the P series papers, we had to offer it at a higher price point due to the change in the manufacturing and milling process.

We trained our consultants at conventions and in our monthly magazine to offer the D and P series options by explaining the differences between the two to their customers. This would help their customers make the right purchasing decisions.

In the spirit of the principle Operating from least to most (you'll remember that from Chapter 4), we did a very limited initial launch of the P series paper. Only a few paper packs were introduced. We didn't know how consumers and our consultants would react to the change in the ISO standard as well as the change in price.

Consultants and customers had always relied on Creative Memories to provide the best-quality products that would not harm their photographs and memorabilia. We were not certain if they would consider the D series paper "good enough" since that is what they had always used. As it turns out, enough people preferred to have the updated quality of the P series paper to justify introducing additional packs. And enough are still quite happy with the D series.

Our obligation now is to ensure that we are still communicating the differences between the two papers, so consumers can make decisions they are comfortable with.

As the field of image permanence continues to grow and evolve, we are committed to staying on top of it or one step ahead. That is our promise to consumers who trust us with their family legacies. That is also our promise to consultants because they need to feel comfortable and confident in the products and programs they offer. We must keep our promise to preserve the quality, integrity, and belief in Creative Memories.

OPPORTUNITY KNOCKS

At Creative Memories, we promote our career opportunity as a chance for women to make money doing what they love. Why women? In the direct-selling industry as a whole, 75 percent of the sales force is female. With Creative Memories, we have about 250 male consultants in our field of 90,000. We welcome men to join our team. The reality is, though, more women do because of our party-plan model and because of their role as family historian. Regardless of gender, we offer a rewarding career for those who embrace and want to share the Creative Memories mission of preserving the past, enriching the present, and inspiring hope for the future through the creation of keepsake family albums.

What does *rewarding* mean to us? Several things really.

First, direct selling gives women the luxury of putting family first. Their established business hours can fit into their family schedule rather than vice versa. This equates to being able to stay home with children during their formative years, being able to be home if someone is sick, being able to volunteer at the school and events of their family, being home when the bus drops the kids off at the end of the day.

The rewards also manifest themselves in the meaningful work that our consultants do. This work is teaching people the importance of preserving their special stories for themselves and for future generations. Consultants offer the researched product and information that supports current standards in long-term photo storage. They provide step-by-step guidance and instruction for completing albums through party plan events (our Home Classes and workshops). And they recognize and reward others for their accomplishments. Our consultants celebrate each album or album page a customer completes. They recognize each stack of photographs that is sorted and organized. Consultants gently encourage their customers to stay committed to their album projects.

Our consultants have helped grieving customers through a loss. They have built a sense of community by volunteering services with local organizations to preserve heritage. They have helped people with mountains of scattered photographs compile a detailed history of their lives.

Consultants also challenge, support, and recognize each other as women, as mothers, and as business owners, and encourage each other to be the very best that they can be without compromising their values and beliefs.

Within their families, our consultants are proud to be role models who are engaged in meaningful work and are bringing home income to support the family's dreams and lifestyle.

Financial rewards are determined by the consultants' goals and efforts. For some, Creative Memories allows them to accomplish short-term objectives—to buy an outfit a month, to be able to be generous during the holidays, to take the family on a once-in-a-lifetime vacation, to be able to reroof the house without taking out a loan or charging it. These are very real scenarios that can easily be accomplished through a Creative Memories home-based business without dramatically affecting the lifestyle choices they have made.

For others, Creative Memories is an exceptionally lucrative business opportunity with limitless income and professional development potential. Doctors, dentists, lawyers, speech pathologists—all successful businesswomen who love meaningful careers but may get burnt out with grueling schedules and demands—have chosen Creative Memories, so they can continue to earn the income equivalent to, or exceeding, what they made in their previous careers while still being able to put their family first.

The beauty of our career plan is that we have options for everyone, regardless of their degree of participation. And we promise to keep it rewarding: personally, professionally, and financially.

To keep this promise, we must commit to continually reevaluating our career plan. This means tracking performance trends to ensure we are still engaging our consultants, whatever their performance goals happen to be. This also means tracking how much we are giving back and reinvesting in them.

Currently, for every sales dollar Creative Memories earns, more than half of it is reinvested in our consultants through commissions, bonuses, rebates, and other benefits. Benefits may be as small (in the spirit of least to most) as free shipping or a product discount, or they can expand to annual growth bonuses and retirement-type benefits. But all aspects of the career plan must be challenging to inspire our consultants to give their personal best. The career plan must be rewarding for consistent activity. And the career plan has to include everyone from the album enthusiast to the career woman.

Why? Less than 10 percent of our field works full time. Album enthusiasts, who work less than 10 hours a week and only make their quarterly minimum $500 ordering requirement, are the majority of our sales force. They enjoy getting their products at a reduced cost and having the ability to share Creative Memories with their family and friends. We cannot overlook them. Nor would we discourage them from being a part of our team. The album enthusiasts represent a significant portion of annual sales, consultant count, and direct contact with consumers. In fact, they may only teach one Home Class every other month. That is their choice. But that one class introduces six to eight new people to the importance of album making. Their main focus is helping family and friends with album projects and hosting the occasional workshop where people can get together and simply work on albums uninterrupted. Their personal motivator usually is the social interaction and living the mission.

The album enthusiasts are as important as the career-minded consultant. Will they receive the same benefits as those who choose to build their home-based business? No. That wouldn't make sense. We do need to match efforts in order to stay afloat as an organization. If we don't have a strong business, our consultants do not have the option of having a strong Creative Memories business. However, our album enthusiasts will receive their product at a discount. They will continue to receive and be inspired by our monthly magazines and new product introductions. And they will continue to be invited to participate in incentive programs and special events like regional conventions if they so choose. They are eligible to expand their business activity and earn additional rewards when they choose to. Creative Memories recognizes and understands, though, that album enthusiasts may not be interested in building a business. Album enthusiasts certainly could change their minds at any time.

Our promise to the career-minded consultant is similar to that of the album enthusiast. Creative Memories provides the same meaningful work. In addition to helping others preserve memories, career-minded consultants help others realize the rewards of home-based business ownership.

Because of this added responsibility, rewards will be greater for higher business activity levels. In addition to teaching Home Classes and conducting workshops for customers, career-minded consultants build a consultant team. As they welcome new people to their unit, they become leaders. Leadership carries the responsibility of training, supporting, and recognizing team members.

Our leaders train their teams how to schedule Home Classes, coach their hostesses, and offer the home-based business opportunity to others. They support their teams through monthly unit meetings, newsletters, and other interaction. And our leaders recognize and celebrate their teams for consistent business activity.

Clearly, our leaders have much more business to juggle than album enthusiasts as they fulfill their personal business activity and their leadership business activity. As a result, we reward them at a higher level. In addition to commissions for personal business activity, career-minded consultants receive commissions, bonuses, rebates, and stipends for their team's activity and for developing other leaders on their team. They also feel the pride and satisfaction of helping others realize their dreams and financial goals.

Another example of the guiding principle "Keeping the promise" in terms of the consultant career is our promise of paying commissions on time every month. Our goal is to process month-end within 3 to 5 days and pay commissions via direct deposit into our consultants' account by the tenth of each month. That way, our consultants can count on their income being available to them by a certain date.

Our promise to all consultants, whether they be album enthusiasts or career-minded, is to continue to offer timely, meaningful work and rewards for sharing the Creative Memories mission with others.

THE MISSION IN MOTION

In addition to our tens of thousands of independent sales consultants, we have over 1,000 employee-owners throughout our organization. They may support the U.S. home office, international business offices, the technology center, publishing and the packaging unit, or one of our manufacturing and distribution facilities. Our employee-owners have a vested interest in the success of Creative Memories and Creative Memories consultants, literally. As employee-owners, they share in the risks and rewards of building an organization. The risks are inherent as we strive to maintain and excel as an industry pioneer—both in the scrapbooking and direct-selling industry. The rewards come from sustained growth in the organization, and they are given in the form of profit sharing, bonuses, added cash flow in the organization, and increased share price for each employee-owner's account in the employee stock ownership plan (ESOP). We are 100 percent ESOP owned and proud of that.

Our promise is to provide meaningful work and a rewarding career for all Creative Memories employee-owners. Our promise is to treat them with dignity and respect. Our promise is also to ensure sustainability, so we have employment opportunities and retirement options for decades to come.

Meaningful work comes in many forms. First, we do everything we can to help employee-owners understand that we are a part of something bigger, something important. We encourage all employee-owners to work on their photo albums. We hold quarterly workshops for our employees. Usually, about 250 of them will show up on a Saturday and work all day on their album projects. We also have a Memory Keepers Club at the home office where employees can work on their albums. On Fridays, departments can reserve the room for team building. As each team works on albums together, they learn more about each other. They connect.

When employees work on their own albums, they understand our product line and how it is used. They can see the importance of quality, instruction, and ease of use.

Once employees complete their first albums, they understand the value of what we do. They feel the joy and pride that comes from album completion. They see the impact completed albums have on others. I've heard from many employee-owners who say their families' lives have been enriched as a result of what we teach.

One woman told me that after more than a decade of marriage, she and her in-laws finally connected. During the holidays a few years back, she asked her mother-in-law if there were any family photos she could look through. Her mother-in-law pulled boxes of photographs out of a closet, and they started looking through them at the kitchen table. Gradually, all the family members came to the table to reminisce. They talked. They laughed. They connected.

Our employee offered to help organize and preserve the pictures in albums. And so they did a little at a time each time the family got together. Now, the relationship is so much more enriched because of the stories that were shared and the time that was spent to preserve the family heritage.

Another employee told me that her parents are finally civil to each other after decades of postdivorce bickering. This employee had spent years trying to find time with both parents during the holidays, and she finally gave up and invited both of them to her house. She laid down some ground rules that said both parents needed to get along, so the holidays were enjoyable for everybody. Her rationale was that after being divorced longer than they were married, they should be able to sit in the same room together and be respectful, at least for a day.

This employee also asked her mother to bring her old Tupperware containers full of family photos that weekend, so they could begin getting the photos in albums. Once this employee and her mother started weeding through pictures, everyone came to the table to learn about the family history. The dad even joined in. At one point, he picked up a picture of the mom from the mid-sixties and said, "You know, Alice Mae, you were a pretty hot little thing."

It was the first time in years the kids had heard either of them say anything nice about the other. And it was the start of happier days to come.

We continually hear stories from our employees of how a completed album helped positively impact their lives. By understanding the value of our mission, our employees know they are engaged in meaningful work. They know that on good days and on bad days, we must do our best at work because we are making a difference in the lives of millions now and for generations to come.

Keeping work meaningful is just one of Creative Memories' promises to employee-owners. And to demonstrate and reinforce this promise, we must encourage our employee-owners to complete their personal albums on a regular basis. They must understand and value the full meaning of our work at the corporation and in the field among our consultants.

EMPLOYEE OWNERSHIP INSPIRES SUCCESS

When Creative Memories solicits feedback from employee-owners on our day-to-day operations and their role in the strategic plan, we are also keeping our promise of providing meaningful and rewarding work. At the same time, Creative Memories is respecting and valuing the expertise that each employee-owner brings to the organization.

The practice of including employees in the day-to-day decision making and strategic planning is not new to our organization. Our parent company, The Antioch Company, was built on this principle. In 1929, founder Ernest Morgan created an operations committee made up of employees to oversee operations. At times, they could and did overrule Ernest's decisions if they felt it was in the best interest of the company and all employees.

As employee-owners, everyone at the company shares in the risks and rewards of growing and sustaining the organization. To that end, we are responsible for soliciting feedback on how we operate from everyone from the executive management team to the employee-owners who operate the binding machines.

Creative Memories and our parent company, The Antioch Company, seek feedback from employee-owners on a regular basis to ensure we are doing our best, day in and day out. We solicit feedback in a variety of ways.

Our improved departmental efficiency and safety (IDEAS) program encourages employee-owners to provide input on our day-to-day operations. Employee-owners can submit ideas that they would like to see implemented. The IDEAS application asks employee-owners to offer their ideas, provide the necessary research (cost savings, improved efficiency, etc.), and submit them for consideration to the IDEAS committee. Ideas can be as simple as having a generic referral card that employees can hand out in lieu of a business card to people who are looking for a Creative Memories consultant. They can also be much larger concepts like starting a new division of Creative Memories, as was the case with our launch of album personalization through custom imprinting on album covers.

Each idea is respectfully considered and sent to the appropriate management team member. The management team member is required to analyze the idea and follow up with the employee-owner who submitted it to discuss the feasibility or implementation of the idea.

The checks and balances of this system is that the idea has to be researched and submitted with cost savings or other impacts on the organization, customers, and consultants. Employee-owners cannot simply submit an arbitrary suggestion without due diligence. The company keeps its promise to engage and listen to employee-owners; however, all employee-owners have to respectfully submit ideas. By doing research, they learn more about the organization, processes, and even coworkers' responsibilities.

Another way Creative Memories receives employee-owner feedback and provides meaningful work is through Great Performances.

Great Performances is our performance management system that allows for continual, 360-degree feedback on an employee-owner's performance. Employee-owners and their immediate supervisors draft an annual plan that outlines major initiatives for the year (a big implementation that will take more time than usual), core job responsibilities (what they are expected to do every day), and development objectives (the skills or training they would like to obtain that year).

Then, they agree on performance measurements that demonstrate achieving, exceeding, or not achieving their plan. And they include sources of measurement. These can include customer feedback, meeting deadlines, and cost savings.

Each person's Great Performance is tied to the company strategic plan, or the big picture. That plan is then translated to major functional areas and what each functional area needs to do to support the strategic plan. Then, each team of that major functional area identifies how it applies to their team. And, finally, each individual documents how they will support that team.

In a very simplistic form, it may look something like this:

The big picture or strategic plan: Creative Memories is the number one source for albums and album-making supplies.

Major functional area: Marketing is responsible for product innovation that will generate excitement and drive sales activity.

Team responsibility: Product development is responsible for being first-to-market in three product categories in 2004.

Individual great performance: I am responsible for introducing one new Custom Cutting System component by the first of each quarter that generates $X in revenue.

The Great Performances documents are dynamic throughout the year. That means employee-owners and their team leaders are encouraged to meet often (daily, weekly, monthly) to touch base on their performance and development objectives. At any time throughout the year, Great Performance plans may change based on a change in business direction, budgeting concerns, and other factors. That is acceptable. The documents provide a starting point, direction, and method for providing regular feedback on performance expectations and fulfillment. Formal midyear and year-end reviews are documented and kept on file.

Birthday meetings are another opportunity to gain employee-owner feedback in an informal setting. Once a month, the CEO, COO, operations managers, or I will gather with employee-owners from throughout the organization who have a birthday to talk in a smaller, intimate setting. We talk about our guiding principles or other corporate values and how they impact us. And we will solicit feedback on what is going well or what recommendations anyone has for improvement. Employee-owners' feedback will be shared with the management team and acted on accordingly. (And, if we can read-dress the Operate from least to most principle here, in conjunction with the birthday meetings, all employee-owners can enjoy birthday treats that we provide in the commons areas. It is amazing how something as simple as a donut or caramel apple can generate excitement. When the announcement is made over the intercom that treats are available, a stampede ensues.)

The passion that our employees have for what we do shows us that we are keeping our promise. We provide meaningful and rewarding work. They wear our logo clothing proudly (and many do every day). And they work on their own personal albums. By doing this, they understand how our product line works from a functional sense. They understand the joy that comes from completing and looking at a family album. And that joy inspires them to do their best each day they come to work.

All organizations have stakeholders: customers, employees, stock-holders, their communities. And we make promises to these constituents each day. The promises may be different for each group. Staying true to those promises is the same. We must keep our promises—of quality, quantity, opportunity, and experience—in order to preserve our relationships with them.

CHAPTER 7

MAKE
IT EASY

❧————————❧

*We are responsible for making it easy for Consultants
to do business with us, for customers to do business with
Consultants, and for employee-owners to perform their
job responsibilities (in that order).*

The fourth guiding principle reaches all the people involved in our
business and focuses on making individual work and work
between individuals as easy as possible. Sometimes making work easy
for one person can make it harder for others. Early on we realized
that we had to establish a hierarchy; we determined that our consultants should always come first, then their customers, and finally the
employee-owners.

Why in that order? Simply put: without our consultants—our volunteer, independent sales force—we wouldn't have a business.

They are our greatest asset. They are our bread and butter, so to
speak. Also, our customer base and our consultant base mirror each
other in demographics and psychographics; therefore, if we keep our
consultants happy, our consumers will more than likely be happy too.
And, ultimately, when they are happy, we will be happy with the sales
and recruiting results they generate.

As our friend Alan Luce, President of the direct-selling consulta-
tion firm Luce and Associates, puts it, "When you have an all-volun-

teer sales force, they are with you because they want to be. They don't have to be. Their own business is not their primary source of income. They believe in the mission, and they have to believe you have their best interest at heart."

One of the many ways we can show that we have our consultants' best interests at heart is to make it easy for them to do business with us. We have to spend more time thinking about the person who unpacks the box rather than the person who packs it. We need to make it easier to place the order rather than take the order, and we need to make it easier to attend the meeting rather than set it up. If we can't make it easy for our consultants to do business with us, then they can't share the mission with their customers, and we don't have a company.

This principle really became important during our rapid period of growth when we almost doubled in size every year from 1990 to 1997. When you go from a $1.1 million organization to a more than $115 million organization, things can get hectic. And employees can get a little tense.

We hire for resiliency—we look for people who don't expect to come to work every day and do the same exact thing in a relatively flat environment. The only consistency we can live up to is consistently evolving to the changing demands of our industries, technology, and workforce. Because of our rapid growth, we are continually hiring new people (as I said, at the end of 2003, more than 69 percent of our employee-owners had been with us less than 5 years), identifying new job responsibilities, implementing new processes, using new technologies, and finding new ways to work together effectively.

Although we hire for resiliency and expect our staff to be flexible, that doesn't mean that in a high-growth state, people don't get frustrated. And in planning meetings—or in water-cooler conversations—we started to hear a great deal about how we could make our employees' jobs easier. How could we cut down the amount of phone calls coming in to check order statuses? How could we decrease the amount of papers going out the door that needed to be proofed? How could we omit the tediousness of keying in fax and mail orders?

The reality is we could. But, whom would we be making it easier for, the consultant or the employee? Yes, we do have to always think about the bottom line and ways to improve our efficiency, productivity, and quality, but the driving force should always be what makes it easier for our consultants and their customers to do business.

So, we have to continually teach our employees that our consultants take priority when it comes to making it easy to do business. At Creative Memories, we incorporate this philosophy into planning meetings by making sure our project leads and management team understand and communicate it. We also incorporate it into presentations that we give at our monthly management and staff meeting. And when we are communicating with our field in print or on stage, we include the Make it easy principle in our message. Since all employee-owners receive our monthly consultant magazine and many employee-owners attend our conventions, they see and hear this message repeatedly.

Now, if we revisit the questions asked above, we would answer our employee-owners this way. How could we cut down the amount of phone calls coming in to check order status? We could implement online order status checking (which we did), but we must presume that some consultants will still choose to call because that is what is more convenient and comfortable for them. Perhaps they have a slow computer or dial-up connection and checking an order online takes too long and is too frustrating. If consultants can make a quick phone call and get fast, friendly service, then why wouldn't they? We will keep that phone option until we reach a time that consultants no longer need it.

How could we decrease the amount of papers going out the door that needed to be proofed? We can post some of them online. But, again, we must factor in those who do not have the comfort or convenience of Internet access (or a good computer). We will provide the ease of print and technology until we reach a time it is no longer necessary.

How could we omit the tediousness of keying in fax and mail orders? We could easily discontinue accepting these. At this time, we choose not to because enough people still find it easy to order this way.

Again, the principle Make it easy applies to our consultants first, customers second, and employees third. Our consultants must be able to quickly and easily learn about new products and programs, obtain the products and materials necessary to share them with others, and sustain their business activity. If they can't reach their customers and they can't reach us, we don't have a business.

GETTING THINGS IN ORDER

The way we accept orders at Creative Memories is often a source of discussion and disbelief for newcomers to the home office. Even though more than 70 percent of our orders come over the Internet (which is a nice little chunk when you factor in 2003 retail sales of more than $400 million), we still accept phone orders, fax orders, and mail orders. In fact, approximately 15 percent of orders are received via phone, 3 percent via fax, and 1 percent via mail.

What about that small 4 percent who choose to use more traditional means of ordering? While we have not opted to discontinue fax and mail orders (which would impact almost 4,000 consultants in our field, not to mention all of their customers), we did implement autoship programs. These programs allow consultants to sign up for an automatic shipment of product at a certain time during the month. They can receive new products when they are introduced, so they have the latest and greatest selection to show their customers without having to go through the motion of placing an entire order.

Consultants can also sign up for status-maintenance orders, so they don't have to think about placing their quarterly minimums in order to remain a consultant. Creative Memories' computer system will automatically send them a minimum ordering requirement every 3 months to keep their account in good standing. The status-maintenance program is more like an insurance policy for them. While they are probably placing monthly orders to support their sales, if they happen to be short—whether it be by $10 or $200—an order will be sent to them to keep them active.

We do have the occasional 20-page fax that is missing pages. We do invest time and money and staffing to key in fax and mail orders. On rare occasions, the mail takes longer to get to us than one may have anticipated. And we do recognize for those consultants who choose to order this way that it will take longer to fill the order because of the manual process involved.

We also accept personal checks in a time when many businesses only accept credit card, money orders, or cash.

Why do we do this? It makes it easy for our consultants to place an order in a way that is convenient *and* comfortable for them. Does it pose some problems? Absolutely. We do have checks being returned for insufficient funds. But we believe it is important for this business to be easy for our consultants. Despite the occasional frustration we may have with the "old-fashioned" way of doing business, accepting checks is what is right for our consultants at this time.

As comfort levels with technology change in the future and as technology continues to evolve (who can predict when facsimile machines will become obsolete?) we will reexamine our business practices and act accordingly.

At Creative Memories, we understand that our approach to business transactions may seem a bit archaic, but our acceptance of faxes, personal checks, and phone orders are appropriate for us.

Several companies choose to strictly have an e-business. Others will accept money orders but not personal checks. Some only accept credit card transactions. Others still, at a local level, may only choose to accept cash. The key to making it easy for people to do business with you is to understand your consumer or your sales representatives. What would make it easier for them? How do they prefer to conduct business? If your consumer base prefers online transactions, then invest your resources to support that.

That being said, don't make decisions that make things easier for consumers if those decisions ultimately harm your business. Our local cinema complex recently switched to a cash-only transaction for moviegoers. The reason? The amount of money they were investing in recovering insufficient check funds was staggering. They opted to only accept cash, put a cash machine in the lobby, and gave the public a 6-month advance notice. While it took some getting used to for those of us who were accustomed to using our checkbooks, we adapted. The cinema is ultimately better off. And one would argue that the consumer is as well because the cost of doing business did not increase as a result of recovering money from bad checks.

SHIPSHAPE

Creative Memories has three manufacturing and distribution facilities in the United States. Each day, these facilities ship approximately 7,000 cartons to our Creative Memories consultants.

The guiding principle Make it easy impacts our order fulfillment from order entry, as you read about earlier, to getting the carton on the doorstep.

First, we ship paper goods: decorative packs of paper, product catalogs, training materials, you name it. Paper goods are really heavy. We have three primary cartons. The carton sizes were determined years ago based on the core products we sell. The main line of products we sell are albums and refill pages, so the dimensions were set up to accommodate the maximum product dimension along with space for void-fill. About 3 years ago we increased the crush strength of our cartons to reduce the amount of product damage we were experiencing during shipment. We have established that the maximum weight that we ship per carton is 50 pounds. This weight was determined more for safety to our consultants and employee-owners rather than what the cartons can handle. Even though we could ship larger cartons, which equates to fewer cartons and less shipping charges, it is not in our consultants' (or employee-owners') best interests because they would be unable to carry the cartons from the doorstep to their dining room table. Lighter boxes make it easier to do business.

Second, we want our consultants' orders to arrive in the best condition. Up until a few years ago, we used heated foam that was placed in cartons prior to taping cartons shut. The foam expanded to the contours of unused space in a carton. Yet, it was easy to use and inexpensive from an operational standpoint. It was not, however, easy to dispose of by our consultants. It had to be recycled, and most refuse companies wouldn't pick it up curbside. Consultants had to make special trips to recycling centers.

Because of the unnecessary burden we were imposing on our consultants, we switched to inflated plastic bags that could easily be cut up and put in regular garbage. An added bonus that our thrifty consultants came up with is that the little plastic bags can even be used for small, personal garbage bags during an album-making workshop for bits of paper scrap or reused by our consultants as packaging protection. The switch to the plastic bags made it easier for our consultants to recycle or to reuse.

IS IT ALWAYS EASIER?

No.

Our consultants inventory our products. That means they have albums and album-making supplies on hand to sell at events or at home if a consumer needs them. We are one of the few direct-selling companies that ask our consultants to do this rather than us shipping products to customers directly. We have selected this option for several reasons.

First, when customers are introduced to Creative Memories at a Home Class (our "party") and complete their first album page with eight of their pictures and journaling, they fall in love. They see their memories come alive on the page and want to continue to complete other pages. Our consultants need to have the product available for those who want to take it home that night and get started with their backlog of photographs and memorabilia.

Once they see how easy and doable it is to complete a scrapbook album page, they can visualize their drawers and shoeboxes full of pictures in completed albums. And, to take it one step further, they can see themselves curled up on the couch paging through the albums on a quiet afternoon with family or friends.

Another reason our consultants inventory product is that you never know when a customer may need an adhesive or decorative element or pen to finish an album. When someone sets aside the time to complete an album, we need to be there to help get it done. If a customer's consultant does not keep an inventory of the essentials for album making (or, as they call them, the "never outs," things like pages, pens, adhesives, page protectors), it might deflate that customer's enthusiasm for completing an album project or that customer might drive to a local retail establishment to get the item.

Finally, our consultants also teach workshops. These events are longer periods of time regularly set aside for people to work on their album projects. Customers come to expect, for example, that the third Saturday of every month, they are going to spend 8 hours working on their albums at Susan's house. Our consultants need to have product on hand as customers need more.

Does carrying inventory make it easy for our consultants to do business? One could argue that it does based on the reasons just listed. It makes it easier for consultants to meet their customers' needs more quickly.

On the other hand, other direct-selling companies ship product directly to the hostess—the person who coordinates an event at her home for family and friends. The hostess then handles sorting through the product and distributing it to her guests. Would this be easier for our consultants? Absolutely. They wouldn't have to receive products, organize the product by customer order, and make sure it gets in their customers' hands. They also wouldn't have to devote a closet or other space in their home to housing inventory between Home Classes and workshops. But would it be the right decision to not ask consultants to inventory product? We don't think so. In this case, making it easy for consultants to do business with their customers takes priority over making it easy for consultants to do business with the home office. When customers get excited about their pictures and stories and commit to completing albums, we want them to be equipped immediately. Creative Memories doesn't want that enthusiasm and that commitment to wane. And we don't want our consultants to have to risk losing a customer. We want them preserving their stories for today and future generations.

RESOURCE ONE

Resource One is another service Creative Memories provides to our consultants to make it easy for them to provide better service to their customers. Resource One allows consultants to buy specific decorative enhancements for their customers on an as-needed basis from the variety packs available in the core line of product.

The Creative Memories Collection offers exclusive decorative paper packs and sticker packs for album makers to enhance their album pages. Within our core collection, we have variety packs. Take the Happenings sticker pack for example. This pack includes stickers that enhance a variety of memory-making moments throughout the year, like birthdays, fall leaves changing color, and the holiday season.

If a customer invests in this pack, he or she has enough decorative enhancements to document a year of memories, almost. There will certainly be enough to complete a few pages each on the holiday gathering, rolling in the leaves, and tending to their flower garden each spring. They may want additional stickers, though, to enhance photographs of every birthday party—rather than just one. But they may not want to invest in another entire Happenings pack.

Resource One provides consultants the opportunity to offer individual sticker strips to their customers. This, in turn, makes it easy for customers to make purchasing decisions that meet their needs and easier for consultants to support those customers. By offering Resource One to our consultants, they do not have to tear open their existing inventory to provide one strip from a variety pack, thus making that pack not sellable.

Is Resource One the best use of our time and money as a company? Not a chance. We do make some money from it. But the logistics of staffing and fulfillment are interesting to say the least. Consultants are not required to order a minimum amount from Resource One on a consistent basis. Their orders are based on customer need. So, it is

difficult to gauge staffing for peak times (which are rare). It is difficult for product development to determine which sticker strips or
paper colors from each pack introduced will be the popular ones that
consumers will want more of. We won't put every sticker strip or
paper color in Resource One. That would equal thousands of SKUs
to house and manage. And, finally, Resource One consumes valuable
resources of time, space, and money that could be better spent elsewhere. Again, though, we do feel offering Resource One helps make
it easy for our consultants to provide optimal customer service.

Sometimes, making it easy for your target market to do business
with you requires that you implement programs and services that are
not the big money makers. As long as initiatives do not lose money
and place your organization in a negative cash situation, the trust,
integrity, and credibility your company gains will strengthen and preserve the business relationships you are building.

BUSINESSMATE

In 2000, we introduced BusinessMate software for our consultants to
provide another way to make it easy for them to do their work. The
software package allows them to manage their contact and downline
information (people who sign up to be on their individual teams)
quickly and easily.

Making the decision to offer BusinessMate was a long process. We
knew that more than 90 percent of our consultants owned and used
a computer. What we didn't know was the comfort level they had
navigating software programs and the confidence they had sending
and receiving business information over the Internet. Finally, we
didn't know how attached they had become to using spreadsheets,
highlighters, paper clips, and all other forms of contact and downline management they had implemented. Sometimes, these habits
are hard to break.

Prior to BusinessMate, our consultants tracked customer contact
information and purchases on index cards, legal pads, and computer
spreadsheets to provide follow-up care. When they wanted to offer

new products in their customers' general preference categories or follow-up on album projects, they had to page through card after card after card (or page after page after page) and manually track their correspondence. They would identify categories (like people who attend my workshops or people who love the 12×12 album size) by different color highlighters, paper clips, stick-on notes, and other visual reference cues. It worked at the time, but could we make it easier for our consultants? Yes. Did they want us to? Yes. Would we agree on what "being easier" looked like? That was up for discussion. Many probably would have been content if we offered colored file folders.

In addition to tracking customer contacts, our consultants also have to track their downline consultant contacts. Downline consultants are people who are on another consultant's team. As discussed earlier, Creative Memories consultants recruit others to help share the Creative Memories mission. Once others sign up to be on a consultant's team (or in their unit), that consultant becomes a leader and is responsible for training, support, and recognition of the team. Leaders train others in selling and scheduling techniques as well as recruiting techniques. Leaders also need to track their teams' monthly activity and productivity rates. By choosing to be leaders, consultants are committed to helping their teams reach specific monthly sales and recruiting activity levels.

In order to do this, our leaders must monitor the monthly activity and productivity of their unit. Prior to BusinessMate, our leaders would receive a monthly report of activity. Now, when I say report, for some it was a two-page document if they had two people on their team. For others, with thousands of people in their unit, they would receive reams of paper. And they would review the report line by line, with different color highlighters, to determine who they needed to recognize for meeting sales goals, who they needed to train, and who they needed to call because they were not meeting quarterly minimums.

BusinessMate software is an essential business tool for leaders. Leaders can schedule ongoing, automatic "refreshes" of their units' activities, so their computers will talk to our computer and get all of the information so the leaders will have the information at their fingertips when they are ready for it. Then, leaders can easily sort information based on what they are looking for. They can quickly retrieve the names of anyone who has not placed a minimum order requirement in the previous months. BusinessMate also provides the functionality to compose a reminder e-mail message to send to those folks and encourage them to order.

Unit member contact information is automatically imported into a consultant's BusinessMate information during the scheduled refresh. Consultants must key in customer contact information, just as they would have to do with any contact management system. While this can be a long, tedious process, the overall BusinessMate software makes it easy for consultants to do business. Currently, more than 9,000 consultants use BusinessMate. Two-thirds of them are career-minded consultants who are building their teams. One-third are consultants with a growing customer base and a vision for leadership.

Making it easy for consultants to do business is at the heart of all we do. It is so ingrained, in fact, our correspondence boasts about it. When we launched the first upgrade for BusinessMate, we used the text shown on the opposite page in our magazine. How many references to the Make it easy guiding principle can you find?

Did you get that it is easy to use?

People can choose to invest money, time, and commitment with any business, any activity, any outlet. To keep them loyal to you and your organization, you must do everything you can to make it easy for them to do business with you. This can range from accepting checks, having ample parking space, not making them wait for service. You name it. If you can afford to do it, do it.

Our third consultant, Leilin Hilde, once said something that summed up the importance of the guiding principle Make it easy. She joined Creative Memories in 1987 and held the title of Executive Director in 2003. She said, "English is a second language to me. I have five kids under the age of 8. And my husband is a minister in rural Minnesota. If I can do this business, anybody can."

It's a bigger, badder, bolder BusinessMate software.

Order or upgrade now for the latest enhancements and additional support

Find out what 6,000 Consultants at all levels of the Career Opportunity are raving about!

Easier communication with customers, Coordinators and fellow Consultants.

Up-to-date recognition and training statistics right at your fingertips.

Effective tools for organizing and managing your time.

If you already own the Creative Memories BusinessMate software, you know how much more efficient running your business can be. If you haven't used BusinessMate software, you don't know what you are missing.

Now, with new upgrades and an easy-to-follow, step-by-step instruction manual, it's even easier to download and use.

New BusinessMate manual available July 1

Creative Memories' new BusinessMate manual provides:

- Easy-to-follow instructions for performing key functions of the software.
- Screen captures that guide you every step of the way.
- Answers to some of our most frequently asked questions.
- Tips on how to get the most out of your software.
- Detailed Table of Contents for easy reference.

You'll learn how to perform an e-mail blast for all of your Home Class Coordinators, so you can share the new Thanks to you!® gifts for the quarter.

Find out how to quickly review your downline's recent business activity in sales and recruiting for newsletter and Unit meeting recognition.

Learn how to record and retrieve your contact history, so you can make well-informed follow-up calls.

It's all in there and more. You'll have 192 pages of step-by-step instruction for the most practical, useful functions in BusinessMate software.

WHAT ABOUT THE EMPLOYEES?

At the Creative Memories home office, we are routinely asked about the part of this guiding principle that says employee-owners are last on the list. Do we not care about employees?

Of course we care. The reality is employee-owners are not last on the list. Our employee-owners are important to the success of our organization just as consultants and customers are. And we do all that we can to provide meaningful, rewarding work for them. Remember, that is our promise.

What the principle Make it easy defines for us, though, is where our priorities lie and where our resources will be allocated when it comes to making business decisions. Ultimately, what makes it easier for consultants and customers to do business is good for the whole of the organization, including employee-owners. We cannot overlook this point. In fact, you will read more about that in our final guiding principle, Ensure sustainability.

For example, our call center staffs approximately 100 full-time consultant service representatives (CSRs) who are responsible for order entry and providing general information to consultants. In 2002, the call center handled over 600,000 phone calls and 149,000 e-mails ranging from "I'd like to place my order" to "Why haven't we been featured on *Oprah*?" Whenever we implement new technology in the call center, there is this common misconception among staff that calls will decrease and life in the call center will be easier.

Although certain categories of calls will be redirected to an automated system, calls, in fact, will not decrease. If we take a look at online ordering, we know this is true. Even though more than 70 percent of our orders are received through the Internet now, call volumes have not decreased. Calls have simply changed focus, and the call center is still handling large call volumes.

If we look at online ordering and test it against the principle Make it easy, though, we find that we did make it easier for consultants and employee-owners to do business even though our focus was on making it easier for consultants. Implementing online ordering made it easier for consultants to do business with us because they could order 24/7. Online ordering also made it easier for CSRs—our employee-owners—to do business because they were able to maintain their service levels and handle call volume. Online ordering offered these employee-owners additional capacity.

Ultimately, what was good for the consultant was good for the employee-owner. The same is true for other organizations. Consider the hotel industry, for example. Even though every room has an alarm clock in it, hotel patrons still call the switchboard to reserve a wake-up call. Why? While I can't speak for everyone, I would assume most of us are not comfortable setting a new alarm clock. Did we properly select a.m. instead of p.m.? Did we actually set the alarm? Are we going to wake up on time for our meeting or our event? By requesting a wake-up call, we receive verification that Ms. Lightle in room 314 will get a wake-up call at 5:30 a.m. We hear it confirmed and are comfortable the call will happen.

Now, many hotels have an automated wake-up service that patrons can call into and type in their request. Even though this system is automated, it still provides the verification of the time, so we can be comfortable with our request.

When we consider the Make it easy principle, we see that hotels provided options for patrons to wake up even though alarm clocks were in every room. And, eventually, hotels implemented an automated system that continued to make it easy for patrons but also opened up some time for employees to provide service elsewhere rather than simply calling every room to wake people up. Ultimately, what was good for the hotel patrons was good for the hotel employee.

On another note, I recently was helping a friend assemble an inexpensive, pressed-wood file cabinet for a dorm room. When we emptied the box, we were pleasantly surprised to see that all the pieces of wood were labeled with a letter. All nuts, bolts, and screws of the same type were packaged separately and labeled as well. And the instructions showed diagram and label references for assembly. What could have been a frustrating time was simple and easy. It took extra effort on the manufacturer's part. The assembly kit needed printed labels, more plastic bags for the presorted hardware, and, I'm assuming, increased worker time to stick the labels on the pieces of wood. Ultimately, though, this extra effort on their part made it easier for the consumer, and this consumer was appreciative. I would definitely recommend that line to a friend with a similar need.

The lesson here is to always stop and think about how to make it easy for others to do business with you. That is the essence of Make it easy. When customers are happy, they return. That, in turn, benefits the company and the employees.

CHAPTER 8

COMMUNICATE CLEARLY AND CONCISELY

We are responsible for providing timely, accurate, and
appropriate communication to all internal and external
partners, setting clear expectations, explaining the "why,"
and communicating change in a positive manner.

Creative Memories believes in timely, accurate, appropriate communication. Why do we do it? We do it for Rosa.

On Monday, March 3, 2003, one of our consultants, Rosa, made a 450-mile trek to St. Cloud, Minnesota, by herself in a blustery snowstorm. Why? It wasn't to pick up an order of the hottest new product. It wasn't to attend a training opportunity at the home office. And it wasn't because she had family and friends here that she wanted to meet with.

To put it in her words, "I just wanted to remember that I was part of something bigger." Rosa is one of the 5,000+ consultants each year who make a pilgrimage to the home office to meet staff and see what we do here.

Rosa has been a consultant since 1996, when she read about the Creative Memories business opportunity in *Good Housekeeping* magazine. She was so moved by our mission that she picked up the phone and called us to become a consultant.

As Rosa puts it now, she currently lives 2 hours away from everything. While she knows there are other consultants in the surrounding area, she relies on Creative Memories' correspondence and events to get reconnected and reenergized with the business.

She realizes that she is in business for herself, but we never want her to feel like she is in business by herself.

Although she is not in the top 5 percent that call themselves leaders, Rosa represents the majority of people who enter into direct sales. As we say, Rosa is a volunteer in our sales force. She isn't with us because she needs to be. She is with us because she wants to be. Rosa loves our product. Rosa loves our mission. Rosa loves knowing that she is part of something that makes a difference in the world.

She may teach the occasional Home Class or workshop for family, friends, and a relatively small but consistent customer base. She may focus on her business a few hours a week. Her main goal, though, is to preserve her family stories in safe, meaningful keepsake albums.

As we develop products, programs, and communication vehicles for the field, it is so important that we remember Rosa. She is who we are trying to reach, support, and encourage.

Every e-mail, every package, every written word, and every one-on-one contact with Rosa helps her remember that she is part of something bigger, something important, something that is changing the world one completed keepsake album at a time.

Everything we do every day helps her share the Creative Memories mission.

To that end, we are responsible for providing timely, accurate, and appropriate communication to our consultants, customers, and employee-owners, setting clear expectations, explaining the reasons, and communicating change in a positive manner. That is the purpose of this guiding principle.

THE DEVIL IS IN THE DETAILS

There is this wonderful quote that states, "Countless, unseen details are often the only difference between mediocre and magnificent."

We tend to agree.

Think of it this way. You are having some family over for dinner, and you ask someone to pick up a few last-minute groceries at the store that you overlooked. Perhaps you asked a spouse, a child, a friend, or a coworker who happens to be running errands.

One of the crucial ingredients you forgot to pick up was milk. This basic ingredient seems simple enough to communicate to someone. Go to the store; pick up some milk. However, the details to communicate that act clearly and concisely are missing. Do you want skim? 2 percent? chocolate? Do you want a half gallon or a gallon? Do you have a brand preference? A bottle preference, as in glass or plastic?

Without those details, we are not going to get the exact result we desire. And the person receiving that communication will feel frustrated, overwhelmed, and lost. We need to ensure that we are providing enough information, on time and in an appropriate manner, to encourage effective communication. We need to think about the other person and what gaps we need to fill in for the person.

When times are going good, it is easy to communicate clearly and concisely. When times are not so good, it is essential.

I remember our little album business doubling every year since 1987. It seemed like we went from $30,000 to over $100 million in such a short time. While we had our challenges, we would always say, "At least we haven't been hit by a bus."

Then came 1997.

We had implemented a new order fulfillment system that would provide greater capacity and growth for the organization. It integrated all of our systems from order entry to shipping. Plus, it provided new functionality that allowed us to provide better information for our consultants as they placed orders and followed-up on orders.

Only a few days after we went live with the conversion, the entire system crashed. We had no means for taking orders, no visibility into the orders already in our system, and no way to track our manufacturing materials.

On top of the computer crisis, we had a new product fiasco that almost seems comical now but wasn't at the time. We had introduced a new album color; it only seems fitting that it was our Creative Memories' logo color sapphire. The orders for it far exceeded what we felt was a lofty forecast, and we had to back order the product.

We were expecting two large shipments of cover material to fulfill album requests. The first truck of book cloth swerved while trying to avoid hitting a deer and capsized in a marshy area. The second truck was hijacked, and its computer equipment and our book cloth were stolen.

And, if that weren't enough, our main shipping carrier went on strike.

In the midst of that, we had our corporate advisory board meeting. I attended wearing a blazer with a t-shirt underneath. The t-shirt had a large tire tread mark across the front and back. I stood up and let them know that the proverbial bus had indeed run us over.

It was in those moments of crisis that we learned the true value of communicating clearly and concisely. Our consultants' personal businesses were at risk, and they wanted to know what was going on. No amount of public relations spinning would save the situation, so we just told it like it was—every detail right down to the truck hijacking.

We let our field know what to expect in terms of order fulfillment time (some were as long as 30 to 45 days); we promised to inform them of any developments, no matter how small; and, of course, we apologized time and again for the disruption we were causing.

After our first communication of the crisis—which I seem to remember being four typed pages—we heard from many consultants in our field. They simply said, "Thanks. Now, we know what we have to work around."

A communication plan was implemented, and our employee-owners received similar communication as we worked to climb out of the mess. We posted bright red 11 × 17 construction paper in common areas throughout the home office and manufacturing facilities. These common areas included lunchrooms and restrooms. (Potty Training 101 is one of the best places to reach a captive audience.)

These were called "hot sheets." Daily, if not more frequently, we would print out messages and post them to these hot sheets.

Sometimes, it was to indicate what progress was being made. At other times it was simply a status update that said nothing had changed, but we were still working on it. Finally, these hot sheets helped quell fears that were generated through the rumor mill, like the company was going to fold. By providing timely, accurate, and appropriate information throughout the crisis, our team knew if something wasn't printed on the hot sheets, it wasn't true. Throughout the crisis, we all knew what was happening (whether it was good or bad) and what we each had to do to help.

Every person, regardless of title or functional responsibility, pitched in. Some packed boxes. Others took orders over the phone onto paper order forms, so we could enter them later. Many were trained on order entry. And once the system was running again, we rented several trailers to put on our front lawn. We filled them with computer stations, and people would work through their breaks, lunch hours, and even stay after hours to make sure the thousands of orders we had taken by hand were input quickly and accurately.

And we came out of the mess bigger and stronger than ever before. I truly believe the strength and the stability came from the clarity and the honesty of our communication. We provided clear information—even though it was not necessarily positive—in a timely manner.

Communicating clearly and concisely doesn't just pertain to big, devastating events like the ones just mentioned. It can apply to simple things like ensuring your customers know that you must receive something by a certain deadline or for clarification. Is the receipt date the day it should be in your hands or is it the postmark date?

Think back to the request for milk that we mentioned earlier. This is a simple act that can easily run amuck without the little details that make a big difference.

Furthermore, communicating clearly and concisely is essential in good times and in bad. If we look back at the dark time in our history when we were hit by the proverbial bus, we needed to communicate often. Interestingly enough, after that difficult time, we became quite good at capacity planning and fulfillment. As they say in business, we have been able to stay ahead of the curve and easily navigate the peaks and valleys of our business. Now, we hear from employees who are concerned that our business is not doing well because they are not having to work overtime as much and they are not operating in crisis mode. Because we had become accustomed to chaos, the calm work environment became cause for concern among employees. Our communication goal then became to reaffirm that we were doing well. We simply became a better, smoother operation.

The lesson here is simple. Communicate clearly and concisely. And communicate often.

Timely, Accurate, Appropriate

Communicating clearly and concisely can mean many different things. First, it means we provide timely, accurate, and appropriate information.

The timeliness of information is crucial. Our goal is to give our consultants ample time to read and digest information before applying it to their business. That way, they do not miss crucial deadlines or feel rushed or worry that they weren't able to participate in an incentive or program.

Our monthly magazine, for example, is scheduled to arrive in consultants' mailboxes before the first of every month. The magazine includes new product introductions, event information, recognition for achievement, incentives, and more.

Without that magazine, consultants do not have the most recent product and program introductions, the current order form, or the incentives that are taking place that month. We drop the magazine in the mail with plenty of time for it to arrive, but it doesn't always happen that way. Our magazine does not always arrive on time. Sometimes, it doesn't arrive at all.

Because we cannot totally control the timeliness of delivery of the magazine other than putting it in the mail by a certain date, we post an electronic version on our consultants' online network. That way, if the mail is late for any reason, our consultants can still access the

Cheryl Lightle was first introduced to direct selling when she was a child. A man came to their neighborhood offering to take pictures of children on his horse. She was delighted by the experience. The experience of that one-on-one relationship is truly what sets direct selling apart from the retail industry.

People underestimate the impact they have on others.

(A) Cheryl's mother, Betty Callaway, taught Cheryl to be strong, independent, and to work hard. She inspired Cheryl to be a survivor.

(B) Wilbur "Web" Holes invented the Webway® photo album in 1938. Consumer loyalty for this album was a catalyst for the creation of Creative Memories.

(C) Ernest Morgan founded his own printing company in 1926 based on his family's Quaker values of sharing and caring. His belief in people and their contribution to a community of work gave Cheryl Lightle the confidence to pursue the concept of Creative Memories.

(D) Ada Kanning, mother of Cofounder Rhonda Anderson, left a legacy of identity and belonging for her children through the keepsake photo albums she taught them to make.

Today, cherished memories are being preserved because of the foundation they laid so long ago.

(A) In 1987, Lee Morgan, CEO of The Antioch Company, uttered three little words to Cheryl Lightle when she asked if she could pursue the concept of Creative Memories. He simply said, "Go for it." Almost two decades later, Creative Memories continues to make a difference in people's lives by teaching others to create safe, meaningful keepsake albums.

(B) At Creative Memories, everyone puts forth their best effort to support Consultants. Here, former Vice President Gina Sonaglia and Cofounder Cheryl Lightle pack boxes to help fulfill Consultant orders that were delayed during a peak ordering time in 1992.

(A, B) Creative Memories Consultants offer Memory Keeping at Its Best.™ This includes products tested for long-term photo storage, researched information, education, and the gentle encouragement to complete keepsake albums. They reach out to customers through Home Classes, workshops, and special events.

(A, B, C) The Creative Memories team of scientists help keep the promise to Consultants and customers. They ensure products comply with current standards for safe, long-term photo storage.

(A, C) Having a sense of fun is integral to the Creative Memories' culture. At Halloween and other special events, employee-owners and Consultants never pass up an opportunity to wear costumes. (B) One Halloween, employees dressed up as Cofounder Cheryl Lightle. As Cheryl says, "Once you've become a costume, you know you've arrived."

(A) Creative Memories began its partnership with the Alzheimer's Association in 2002 to help preserve memories, identity, and a sense of belonging. In 2 years, Creative Memories Consultants raised more than $1 million for Alzheimer's research and education.

(B) Million-dollar milestones are only a few of the causes for celebration at Creative Memories. Family day, the winter season party, album-making workshops, birthday treats, potlucks, and picnics are frequent and festive. Cofounders Cheryl Lightle and Rhonda Anderson and first employee Susan Iida-Pederson show off Creative Memories' cake from 1990, its first million-dollar year.

Creative Memories World Headquarters and Technology Center (A) is located in St. Cloud, Minnesota. Facilities in (B) St. Cloud; (C) Sparks, Nevada; and (D) Richmond, Virginia, manufacture and distribute Creative Memories products to Consultants in the United States, Canada, and around the world. The publishing facility in (E) Yellow Springs, Ohio, prints and packages materials and products in the Creative Memories Collection.®

information they need to place their orders on the first of the month and plan their sales and recruiting goals for the month.

Accuracy is also essential. Deadlines, product pricing, availability dates, numbers printed for sales and recruiting recognition, names—all of these things need to be accurate. If they are not, the company loses credibility. People question if we are paying attention, if we have our act together, even, if we actually care about the consultant.

Providing inaccurate and inconsistent information poses many problems for our consultants. Consultants become confused. This leads to increased phone calls for clarification. People miss deadlines or qualifications and become frustrated, and we spend a lot of energy and money cleaning up the mess. It's so much easier to just get things right the first time. That takes processes, patience, good editing skills, and accountability.

Spelling is also an element of accuracy. I'm always puzzled by spelling errors in print, particularly on billboards. Billboards usually only have 6 to 10 words on them. You'd think people could get them right. A bank in town had a billboard across the highway from our office that said "Banking at it's best." It took almost 6 months for the apostrophe to be taken out. And they just covered it up. They didn't move the "s" over and completely fix the sign. Misspelled words really make an organization look careless. At Creative Memories, coincidentally, our tagline is Memory Keeping at Its Best. We have sent out a number of e-mails to our staff and consultants on how to correctly punctuate and use the tagline. We have an image to uphold.

While a spell checker is a nice tool to use, it does not catch everything. Recently, in our employee newsletter, we were highlighting an employee and her job. One aspect of her job is to "assess" training needs. The word was not keyed in correctly, and I'm sure you can guess what word was actually printed. Needless to say, she did get a lot of inquiries about her day-to-day responsibilities.

A few years ago, our communications department manager gave out a mug to her team that said, "Perfection is our goal. Excellence will be tolerated." At Creative Memories, our goal is to achieve 100 percent accuracy in our written correspondence; realistically, we usually achieve about 98 percent. Considering we have thousands of documents, packages, and Web pages that we create each year, that leaves a lot of room for improvement. Out of every 100 pieces that we write, two may have an error. We keep working for perfection; for now, excellence will be tolerated.

We do have some prioritization, though, in our tolerance for errors—the things we can let go of or stress over. Our consultants' names should never be misspelled. That is inexcusable out of respect and appreciation for all that they do. If given the choice of only correcting one thing on a final press proof, it should always be a consultant's name. Pricing, deadlines, and product specifications are at the top of the priority list, as well. Consultants need this information to effectively operate their businesses.

Again, we strive to be 100 percent accurate. But we also recognize we are humans in a fast-paced environment. We do the best we can. We aim for perfection and tolerate excellence.

The final key to communication, appropriateness, is one of the most difficult things to teach someone in writing. Ultimately this means that the tone and voice of a message can have incredibly negative effects on a relationship, personally and professionally.

One of the first aspects of appropriateness in communication is that we must assume the best, always. Our business is a relationship business. I'd argue all businesses are a relationship business. We must do everything we can to preserve the relationship. By assuming the best about other's intentions, motives, and communication style, we can do that. Think about a time when you've received a note from your bank, your public utilities, a school—anywhere—that let you know something was late. There's an appropriate way and an inappropriate way to convey that message.

The inappropriate way would be, "Ms. Lightle, Your electric bill is 10 days late. If we do not receive payment by October 30, your lights and heat will be shut off."

To many people, this is acceptable. It communicates a message clearly and concisely (that's our guiding principle, right?). It also provides timely, accurate information. They haven't received payment. The electricity will be turned off by October 30.

What it doesn't include is an appropriate message that preserves our relationship. I live in Minnesota. It gets cold at the end of October. I need my electricity. The message shows they obviously don't care about me. (I, of course, assumed the best about the electric company. They weren't trying to sound mean. They simply did not have the skills to write a friendly letter.)

An appropriate letter would assume the best of me and work to preserve the relationship with a gentle reminder. I actually received this note when I missed payment because I was on an extended business trip. Notice the difference in tone and the positive attributes: "Ms. Lightle. Perhaps you accidentally overlooked your bill this month. We'd love to hear from you. If this message crossed paths with your payment in the mail, please disregard it and have a great week. If you haven't yet sent payment, please do so by October 30. We appreciate your business."

The company assumed I may have simply forgotten or overlooked my bill. That doesn't make me out to be a bad person. They welcomed me to send the payment, even though it was late. They said please. They acknowledged that it may have been held up in the mail. And, finally, they said they appreciated doing business with me. How cool is that? And I owed them money.

I recognize that some correspondence needs to cut the ties between a business and a consumer or a company and an employee or between two people. These can still be written with directness. And they can still be respectful.

Some helpful hints:

1. Offer a warm opening.
2. Present facts and options objectively.
3. End on a positive note.

We have a deactivation letter that we have to send to those who can no longer be consultants for any number of reasons. Perhaps they simply wanted to resume their relationship as a customer. Perhaps they recently had a child and wanted to focus on being a parent. Perhaps they had to leave the country on military assignment and couldn't operate their business from that particular international location. While this letter is the official announcement that our business relationship no longer exists, we make every effort to be polite, honest, and respectful of the consultant–home office relationship we once had. We want to continue to have a Creative Memories–customer relationship with the individual. We want them to remain committed to preserving their family stories.

Deactivation Letter

Dear _____,

Every Creative Memories Consultant is an important and necessary part of sharing our mission to preserve our precious family photos and stories. You have touched hundreds of lives through your Home Classes and Workshops, and we at the Home Office and your upline are available and ready to help you continue this positive and valuable work.

We understand that there are times when a Consultant chooses an inactive status, and we also know that sometimes this occurs unintentionally. Whichever situation applies to you, we are ready to help you remain an active part of Creative Memories. In reviewing your business activity, your account records indicate that you were unable to meet the qualifying minimum order requirement in the last three months. As a result, your account became inactive **August 1, 2____**. *(Reactivation is necessary if you wish to attend upcoming Company Sponsored events and receive Company mailings.)*

To reactivate easily, please call a Consultant Service Representative today at 1-888-227-6748. You can bring your account up to active status with a minimum retail sales order of $500 (500 QV in Canada) and a $50 reactivation fee. With these items ready and just one phone call, you can continue growing your business and helping people preserve the past, enrich the present and inspire hope for the future.

If this is your **first** time deactivating and you reactivate **before August 22, 2____**, your downline Consultants *can* remain in your downline. If you are unable to reactivate by the deadline above or this isn't your first deactivation, your downline will permanently bump up to your upline. Please reference the Repromotion policy based on your title prior to your inactivation.

Consultants without downline can reactivate any time within the six-month period (less than six months from the deactivation date). Reactivating after six months qualifies you as a New Consultant. You will then need to sign a new agreement, purchase a new training kit, choose an upline and can take part in the 90 Success Plan.

Thank you for being an important part of Creative Memories. We hope that you choose to continue your valuable work of sharing our mission and message with those around you, and we truly want to hear from you soon. We are waiting for your call!

Notice how the first paragraph validates the work they have done as a consultant. It also reminds them that the home office and their upline are here to help them in their business.

The subsequent paragraphs outline the details of what happened in objective, nonthreatening language. We could have said, "You didn't place your minimum order, so you have been deactivated." Instead, we focused on the fact that whether their inactivity was by choice or accidental, we understand. And we provide complete detail for reactivating.

The ending lets them know that we would love to have them back on our team. It preserves the relationship and communicates in a way that is appropriate for showing them what is going on while still respecting them.

Assuming the best also positions consultants and customers in a positive, inspiring light. When we introduce incentives or offer a Creative Memories career to others; for example, we assume they want to and are able to achieve the goals and qualifications outlined. We demonstrate this in our language. If a consultant needs to reach a certain sales threshold, we assume she or he will when we outline qualifications and rewards.

Consider these two statements for a moment:

1. If you reach $1,800 in sales in December, you will receive a Creative Memories logo watch.

2. When you achieve $1,800 in sales in December, you also earn a
   Creative Memories logo watch.

The first statement is clear, concise, and appropriate. It gives the
amount of sales needed to receive a watch. But, the word *if* positions
the incentive as an option for consultants, something they may want
to or may be able to achieve. The word *reach* implies that they will
have to stretch to achieve the goal.

The second statement assumes the consultant will earn the incentive. It immediately informs the consultant that *when* she achieves the
incentive she will also *earn* the watch.

When we assume the best about people, we will be more produc-
tive rather than being angry, confused, or frustrated. Besides, assuming the best—rather than accusing of the worst—is the trademark of
a good partner and a true friend.

Appropriateness also impacts the angles, examples, and positioning
we use in advertising, speeches, and publications.

A few years ago, we had a year-long incentive called A Trip Down
Memory Lane. Each quarter, we celebrated a different decade in our
promotional materials by highlighting historical events. In the final
quarter of the incentive, we focused on current events. At the time,
we had just completed the notorious 2000 presidential election that
shed some less-than-favorable light on Florida.

In the promotional materials for that quarter, we wrote some
tongue-in-cheek humor about making sure everyone's vote counted,
that they should redeem their incentive points online to avoid dim-
pled chads, etc. While this was clever and current, it was highly inappropriate for us. And we got a few calls from our consultants in
Florida who were disappointed in our choices.

I have to agree with them. And we should have known better. We
know that we won't always please everybody in our product and program choices. But if we can avoid deliberately offending someone
simply for the sake of humor, let's avoid it. Why damage your credibility needlessly?

The only way you can know what is appropriate is to know your
audience. Who are they? What do they value? What lifestyle choices

do they make? What magazines do they read? What is a typical day like for them? What motivates them? What disappoints them? Answer these questions, and you will know what is appropriate.

On the flip side of this, don't make apologies for who you are. We had a consultant send us a magazine article in 1997 from *Cosmopolitan* that had the headline, "Kick a— career moves." She said she would love for us to offer recruiting materials written in this way; however, she recognized it probably wasn't appropriate for our consultant base.

She encouraged us to secure some editorial consideration in *Cosmopolitan* because Creative Memories ". . . offered a career that truly was kick a—," and we should tell the world about it.

That being said, we welcome *Cosmopolitan* to share our career opportunity with their readers in a way they feel appropriate, in a way that speaks to their readership. We would love to see their positioning of what we do. In our materials, however, we will continue to offer the phrase "meaningful work."

Meaningful work is the appropriate phrasing that we communicate to our consultants and our customers. It fits their style and their comfort level. Do we have consultants on our team who wouldn't be offended by phrasing it the *Cosmopolitan* way? Sure. But they are not the majority. We must communicate clearly and concisely for the masses.

NEVER SAY NO—PROVIDE OPTIONS

At Creative Memories, we never say no—at least we avoid it at all costs. We may say we are unable to do something at a particular moment. We may provide alternative options for somebody. We avoid saying no.

What does this mean? Part of protecting relationships (which we'll focus on in Chapter 9) is finding alternative solutions that work for all parties. We do have policies that we adhere to for legal reasons and business reasons, but we do have to ensure we are doing our best to help people out, even if we cannot fulfill their original request. While the ultimate outcome is that we cannot do something (a "no" response to an activity), our approach to answering a request is to provide options and explain our reasons.

For example, occasionally, we will get calls from consultants who want to join someone else's team. For whatever reason, they are not satisfied with the person they signed up under (their upline). We can't fulfill this request for a very serious reason. If people started changing their lineage (the team they are on), we would not be able to track activity and pay out commissions and bonuses.

Do we say no? Not quite. We say we are unable to help them with their request at this time. And we give them options. We ask them to go directly to the source and try to work things out with their upline. We ask them to operate their business independently and not be so worried about that relationship if it is that stressful for them. We let them know that they can deactivate for 6 months and sign up under somebody else. After 6 months, our systems would be able to recognize them as a new consultant.

The reality is that switching uplines (changing whose team a consultant is on) would be a quick fix. It is not necessarily the correct option. So we help them find solutions that are right for them and respect their choices.

I've often wondered what a world without *nots* would look like. How would we treat each other if we shared what we could do rather than couldn't do? How would we advance if we offered options rather than simply saying no? How would we feel about ourselves if we didn't immediately default to "I can't do that"?

To illustrate what I mean, consider the common sign that says, "Don't walk on the grass." Why can't we focus on the positive and say, "Please walk on the sidewalk?"

If we focus on what is positive, what is possible, what is polite, we'd all be a little better off with ourselves and each other.

GIVE THE "WHY"

As adults, we often laugh (and sometimes sigh) at the inquisitiveness of children. Why is the sky blue? Why do I have to eat vegetables?

Why are you the boss of me? We can answer many of these, which will most often lead to another "why" question. Sometimes, we simply have to admit we just don't have all the answers.

I'm not sure when it happens, but we eventually get to a point when we stop explaining the "why" behind a decision or an activity. We even stop thinking about the "why." A friend of mine has two little boys. And the boys often ask to have a sleepover. A sleepover can mean having friends over, or it can simply mean that the family goes to sleep in one of the other family member's room.

The rule has always been that they don't have sleepovers on school nights. The reason is simple, and anyone who has kids can relate. Kids don't sleep in one spot. At any time during the night you can have a foot in your face, an elbow on your leg, and a body perpendicular to your stomach. I'm not sure how the kids sleep through that, but parents certainly don't. So school night sleepovers are out.

One weekend, though, the boys asked if they could have a sleepover in the living room. My friend immediately said no without thinking about it. The kids, of course, pressed on. "Why not?" they asked. The only answer my friend could come up with was that she was tired and didn't feel like hauling the pillows and blankets to the living room and getting everything set up. That was not a good enough reason for the boys. The boys kept pressing on, with promises to help prepare the living room and clean up in the morning. My friend ultimately realized she was saying no simply because she was tired. When the boys forced the issue and caused her to rethink the sleepover, she realized that with everyone pitching in to help, a sleepover could happen easily. It did. And they ended up having a wonderful time.

Even though that is a simple example of stopping to think about why we do some of the things we do, it does illustrate the point. We need to stop, think, and explain our reasons for doing things. Too often we rely on or revert to what has always been done or what is easiest. Sometimes, we simply need to rethink our position. Perhaps we will stick to our decisions or actions. Perhaps we will change. At least we are getting to the root of why we do things.

Now, back to my point. As adults, we don't typically communicate the "why" unless we are asked (or, as in the case with parents, we are hounded by our children to provide further explanation). That should change. By offering explanation, we offer understanding. We may gain others' agreement. We may hear an alternative. But we owe it to each other to, as Stephen Covey says in his *7 Habits of Highly Effective People*, "seek to understand before being understood." People will respond more favorably if told why.

This rule applies in life and in business.

For us, at Creative Memories, our guiding principles often are the reason why we do things. And, as I said earlier, these guiding principles help ensure consistency in decision making and communication from the home office. They apply to almost all things we do.

When we are presenting expectations, for example, in our career plan or in special incentives to drive business activity, we have a lot of explaining to do. We don't want people to think we are arbitrarily assigning qualifications to them. All numbers represent specific business activity. And all rewards are awarded based on different levels of business activity.

For instance, if an average Home Class yields $300 in sales, sales goals will be listed in increments of $300. So, if a consultant is interested in earning a sales consistency bonus, she will have to place $1,200 in personal sales volume each month for 3 months in a row. This assumes that she is teaching four average Home Classes a month, each month, for 3 months in a row. She will earn a bonus for consistently teaching Home Classes.

Now, to take this example a step further, we are often asked questions like, "Why can't I get the consistency bonus if I have a total of $3,600 in 1 month? It's the same level of activity." That's a great question. The answer is simple. Yes, $3,600 is the same dollar amount as $1,200 each month, 3 months in a row. However, rewarding for $3,600 in 1 month is different than rewarding for $1,200 in a month, every 3 months.

Commissions will be about the same reward on both examples because of the dollar value. But the consistency bonus rewards consistency, not just dollar value. So a consultant may have a good month and sell $3,600 in product. That is great. Keep up the great work. We celebrate and acknowledge your achievement through the standard commission awards. The sales, however, do not reflect consistency.

Each reward is tied to a specific, clear business activity. And we don't reward twice for the same activity. We want people to stretch. Rewards inspire them to stretch and do more than they usually do each month. Commissions reward for sales in a given month. The consistency bonus rewards for the same level of activity month after month after month.

Sales and recruiting incentives will also be set at higher levels of business activity than the norm. Why? Because they are incentives. They are designed to inspire people to stretch to new heights. They are not offered as something for everybody. Can everyone choose to participate? Yes. Does everyone? No. And, as we said earlier in this chapter, when we offer these incentives to everyone, we assume the best of them. We assume everyone will want to earn the incentive. We assume everyone is capable of earning the incentive. We assume everyone will earn the incentive. And we offer the qualifications and rules in a timely, accurate manner, so all consultants can choose to participate.

Whenever we launch a new incentive (be it a year-long campaign to win a trip or a monthly incentive to earn free product), we instantly hear from people who say the incentive just cannot be earned. It is too hard. It is unmotivating. The reality is, it's not. Consultants earn these trips every year. And we need to communicate that often.

We respect that opinion. We respect that choice to not participate in an incentive (that is also one of our guiding principles, Respect personal choices, which you will read about in Chapter 9). And, each time we offer an incentive, we are pleased by the number of people who choose to stretch themselves and succeed by earning the reward.

Creative Memories also offers *inclusive* and *exclusive* awards. Inclusive awards are awards that anybody can earn. They could include welcoming a specific number of consultants to your team. They could include a specific sales goal. The minimum requirement will still cause someone to stretch their business goals, but anybody can earn the award. It is open to include anyone who wants to try and achieve it. Exclusive awards are limited, like a top-10 category for sales, recruiting, or development. Only 10 people can earn the award; therefore, it is exclusive.

We offer both inclusive and exclusive awards so more consultants have the opportunity to participate and be recognized for the achievements. If we only offered a top-10 category, only 10 people would be celebrated. We want to recognize and celebrate as many consultants as we can as often as we can. That being said, we respect if our consultants choose not to take part in the incentive offered.

We are also pleased by the number of people who chose to participate but didn't quite achieve their goal. Why? Because they recognized the opportunity and committed to going for it. Even though they didn't reach their goal, their business is stronger because of the increased activity level and their renewed enthusiasm. In addition, the next incentive will be easier for them. If you think about baking a cake or playing tennis, it is hard the first time. There's so much to learn and remember. Each time you repeat the activity, you get better at it. The likelihood of success increases each time.

Not everyone will be happy with the answers they receive for why something is done. The goal is not to make everyone happy. The goal is to provide the answers to try and help everyone understand.

TAKE IT TO THE SOURCE

One final way that we can commit to communicating clearly and concisely is to take issues, concerns, and questions to the source of our angst, confusion, or question.

I'm often amazed when people come to me to express frustration about somebody or something that happened. My first question always is, "Did you talk to them about it?" Unfortunately, the answer is usually no.

At Creative Memories, we understand that a key part of communicating is to live by the rule Take it to the source. If you are having an issue with somebody, if you are frustrated or offended or have mis-understood something somebody said, go talk to them. Work it out together. Talking to somebody else is not going to solve the problem.

I think people avoid taking problems to the source because they are afraid of conflict; they are afraid of being vulnerable. We need to get over that and simply talk. What's the worst that could happen?

Back when Creative Memories first started, we were trying to trademark the name of our program Shoebox to Showcase. We were told we couldn't because it potentially violated the intellectual prop-erty of a major greeting card company. I personally disagreed. They offered greeting cards. We offered photo albums.

Well, our lawyers got in touch with their lawyers and decided that for $60,000, we could probably work out a deal. But this was unacceptable to me. We were new and didn't have the money to throw around on the possibility of being able to keep our name. So I decided to go directly to the source and bypass the lawyers. I called the company and got in touch with one of their vice presidents. And after I explained what it was that we were doing, we had the company's blessing.

Creative Memories could have haggled this out with attorneys, but that would have just got in the way.

In another instance, one of our managers spoke negatively about a vice president during a very difficult time in their working relation-ship. Another employee overheard the comment and informed the vice president what had been said.

Once the manager and the vice president calmed down a little bit, they got together to talk it out. They discussed the inappropriateness of the comment. They discussed the actions and emotions that lead to the comment. And they discussed what they both could do to work together better for the sake of themselves, their team, and the organization. Was it easy? Absolutely not. It's never easy to start a conversation with, "So, I heard you called me a . . ."

Voices were raised. Wholesome word choices were not always used, but perceptions and expectations were laid on the table and dealt with. Both of them, and their teams, came out better as a result. Are the manager and vice president friends now? I wouldn't go that far, but they have an understanding and appreciation for each other's position.

Go directly to the source. Seek to understand them. Ask questions like, "What did you mean when you said that?" Or let them know, "In today's meeting, you did . . . This is how I interpreted it. Is that what you intended?"

Then, help others understand where you are coming from.

Find common ground (like doing what's in the best interest of your customers or finishing a project on time or under budget). You'll save time, money, and energy and strengthen your relationships.

These concepts apply to employees, as well, as we discuss performance expectations, reasons for decision making, and options for growth and development.

There's no greater gift we can offer our employees and teams than to effectively communicate job descriptions, responsibilities, and expectations. Communicating clearly and concisely alleviates any anxiety about what is expected of individuals and empowers them to initiate action in their day-to-day work. In its simplest terms, the principle "Communicate clearly and concisely" takes the job responsibility "handle customer inquiries" and transforms it into clear, concise expectations. A clear, concise revision could be, "Answer all customer inquiries with timely, accurate, appropriate order information within 24 hours of receiving their call, fax, or e-mail." This revision explains what it means to "handle" an inquiry, what type of information to provide customers, and what the expectation is for a prompt response.

Offering reasons for decision making also empowers employees. Much like the Creative Memories guiding principles, explaining reasons and rationale to employees can help drive decision making down, so employees, too, can make decisions in their day-to-day work consistent with corporate or executive philosophy. Helping employees make sound business decisions is part of effective succession planning, too, as upcoming leaders learn to weigh the impact of their decisions on the organization.

What better way to strengthen all of our relationships than to communicate clearly and concisely. Provide timely, accurate, and appropriate communication always. Assume the best. Never say no; provide options. Take it to the source. And explain your reasons for doing things.

If you are not sure where to begin, start by conducting all your meetings at the honesty table. At the honesty table, everything is laid on the line. People have permission to express what they are concerned or confused about. And, as members of the honesty table, everyone has to reciprocate by not being offended and helping to provide clarity or solutions.

All of these tactics contribute to strong, successful internal and external relationships within an organization. And, as I said before, all businesses are relationship businesses.

CHAPTER 9

PROTECT THE RELATIONSHIP

⤜⟐⟐———⟐⤛

*Creative Memories Consultants, consumers, and
Home Office staff are interdependent. We have mutual
responsibilities to ensure growth, sustainability, and success.*

*We are also responsible for preserving the direct-selling
relationship between Consultants and customers. All of
our actions (with technology, promotion, method of
distribution, etc.) must direct consumers to a Consultant.*

US, NOT US AND THEM

We need each other. It's that simple.

Our customers need their consultant. The number of people we meet who have years of photographs and memorabilia stashed away in shoeboxes and drawers is staggering. For most of them, they don't know where to begin. They don't have the time. They don't think they have the skill or the will to get their pictures in documented photo albums.

That's where our consultants come in. Creative Memories consultants teach the importance of memory preservation. They offer the best tools available in the marketplace in terms of quality and ease of use. And they offer hands-on instruction and encouragement for step-by-step, box-by-box completion of safe, meaningful keepsake albums.

Our consultants need their customers. If their customers don't understand the importance of memory preservation and commit to completing albums, consultants don't have a job. They have wonderful tools (a meaningful mission, Home Classes, albums, and album-making supplies), but a tool is only good when put to use.

An old acquaintance of mine named Mardee Thomas uses this wonderful chain saw example when she offers sales training. She says, "You can buy the most amazing chain saw on the market. It can be gas powered, have a heavy-duty blade and all of the safety mechanisms needed. But, if you bring it out and set it next to the tree, it's not going to do the job. A tool cannot perform by itself. You have to pick up that chain saw and make the cut yourself."

Our consultants can have the most amazing tools for their business, but without sharing those tools with customers, the tools do not have value.

Our independent sales team needs the home office to provide the best product, program, and career plan to help ensure their growth, sustainability, and success.

If we don't provide both a product and a program that they can believe in—that generates excitement for them—they won't offer it to others. If we ask them to build a team and we don't provide them with the tools, the direction, and the compensation to make it worthwhile, they won't do it.

If we implement business practices or operate in a manner that is not in the best interest of the field as a whole, we won't have the money to reward them or the ability to carry on. They will quit, or, worse yet, we'll all lose our jobs.

As a result, we must use due diligence before making change. Our consultants can choose to go to any direct-selling company. They choose Creative Memories because they love the mission and trust our support. We cannot ever lose that trust.

And, we need them—our consultants and our customers. Let's face it, we are a for-profit business. If consultants are not teaching Home Classes, they are not fulfilling the role of direct selling. If consultants are not placing orders to fill customer needs, we are not generating income. If we are not generating income, we cannot reinvest in our consultants and our company.

We would cease to exist.

IT'S ALL IN THE NAME

To help continually remind us of this interdependent relationship, we opted to define our roles differently. In the early 1990s, we changed the name of our customer service department to "consultant services." While this may seem minor, it changed our perception of our role and the way we interact. As Stephen Covey teaches, we have an interdependent relationship. We each bring something to the table.

Prior to the name change, we would often be reminded by our consultants that the customer is always right. Therefore, if they had an issue with an order or an opinion to share, we should simply listen and offer everything we could to remedy the situation.

By changing the name to consultant services, it brought awareness to the relationship we have as a direct-selling company. We have a responsibility to offer the best product, program, and career. Consultants have a responsibility to offer these things to their customers. And we both have to work together to do the greatest good for the greatest number.

We also changed the name of our corporate office from the "corporate office" to the "home office" in 1999. Too often, when we were on the road meeting with consultants, we would hear, "Oh, you're from corporate." Or we would be introduced as "This is corporate." Now, that's not very warm or relationship-oriented is it?

It really strained relationships and put this aura of "us" and "them" into play. It had staleness about it, an unemotional lack of appeal. It sounded cold and distant.

As the home office, we are our consultants' home away from home. We welcome them to come and visit. We hope our office is one of comfort and direction. We, as employees and consultants, are family. We have struggles. We have successes. We work together to overcome crises and to celebrate achievements.

We have names. I am Cheryl. Yes, I carry the title of cofounder. But, I am simply Cheryl. Talk to me. I am human.

It's in the best interest of all organizations to define and understand the interdependent relationships they have with employees, customers, vendors, you name it. We can all find success if we understand what each of us brings to the table, and we all respect what others bring.

It's not about "us" and "them." It's about us.

OUR SALES FORCE AND ITS CUSTOMERS

We've been through the industrial age and the technical age. Now, I see the people age.

Our society has become very automated, but I don't believe that inanimate objects can make decisions and motivate people. That's what direct selling is about—building relationships that motivate, educate, and celebrate.

Creative Memories is perceived by some as a photo album manufacturer. And we are the largest domestic photo album maker. But we are so much more than that. Creative Memories offers meaningful, rewarding opportunities for our consultants, our hostesses, and our customers. We are about building relationships that transcend business transactions. And relationship-building is what is at the heart of direct selling.

According to the Direct Selling Association, several hundred thousand people join the industry each week. This growing trend of people embracing direct-selling opportunities will continue. I view this as society searching for the high-touch aspect of personal service in a world that has become increasingly technological. While medical advancements, Internet proliferation, and telecommunication developments change at lightning speed, people are searching for personal interaction, support, and encouragement. Direct selling provides this.

While we, as consumers, may embrace online banking, grocery shopping, and other forms of e-commerce, we still want to know someone out there that cares about who we are and what we do. So, as consumers, whether we are investing in keepsake albums, cosmetics, kitchen utensils, baskets, or telecommunications, we want our direct-selling consultant to know we are more than just a business transaction. We want to trust their guidance, recommendations, and belief in the products and the services they offer. We want to know they care about our purchasing decisions. This will become increasingly important as technology continues to keep us from face-to-face contact.

Creative Memories consultants provide this one-on-one relationship with their customers. They do what nobody else can do: Our consultants create an unmatched experience for our customers that is unequaled by any retail store. Creative Memories consultants build relationships. They encourage and gently nudge album makers along. They know about their customers' families. They relive vacations with their customers. They help them through heartache. They help them dream. They help them get their memories and stories into albums. They help them love life. This cannot be equaled anywhere in the retail world.

And we must do everything we can to protect that relationship.

People can buy photo albums and album-making supplies anywhere. We know that. People cannot find our consultants' service and relationships anywhere. That is more than our competitive advantage. That is who we are.

When we say our tagline, Creative Memories offers Memory Keeping at Its Best, we are referring to more than just the highest-quality product and program and mission. We are talking about our consultants and how they relate and support their customers. We cannot ever damage that trust, that integrity, and that priceless relationship.

As we continue to grow and are faced with technology and opportunities that could easily generate new business for Creative Memories, we must remember that our consultants are Creative Memories. We cannot bypass them. We cannot make business decisions that are detrimental to them. We must keep them at the forefront of everything we do. In the early 1990s we were at a crossroads in our business, and the guiding principle "Protect the relationship" took center stage.

At that time, we were only 3 years old and hadn't invested in our product line. Our consultants offered Webway photo albums through the direct sales channel. It was all that we had for this start-up business and new venture into direct selling. Unfortunately for our consultants, Webway photo albums were also available in retail stores. While it made sense to use existing product for our initial launch of the company (again, this relates to the guiding principle Operating from least to most—use the resources you have on hand first), we had come to a point where we needed to distinguish between Webway products and Creative Memories products for the sake of our consultants. We needed to make a commitment to invest in and proceed with building this new business. Our consultants were losing faith that we were committed to Creative Memories and our consultants' best interest because the product they were asked to sell was available in the retail sector. They didn't have their own product to get excited about.

Developing exclusive product for Creative Memories was difficult for me, personally, because I had been brought into Webway as vice president of marketing. And I was charged with finding a way to revitalize the bankrupt business. The vision for Creative Memories really changed all of our plans and our focus. The concept of direct selling was new to us. Creating an entire new line of photo-safe products was new to us. The idea of personalized scrapbook photo albums was new to us. But we were determined. Despite the uncertainty of our new business venture, I often turned to this quote by philosopher Joseph Campbell for inspiration, "We must be willing to get rid of the life we've planned, so as to have the life that is waiting for us."

And we did.

As Leilin Hilde, one of our first three consultants, remembers, "Cheryl really stood up for Creative Memories consultants at that time. She was instrumental in getting us product differentiation, exclusivity, and price parity. She has looked out for us from the beginning."

We launched a new line of scrapbook albums that had different sizes, pages, cover materials, and functionality than the traditional pocket-page albums Webway was known for. It was a limited launch, only a couple of albums, but it was the start of our commitment to an exclusive product line that is only available through Creative Memories consultants.

Our consultants' enthusiasm and trust grew. So did our program. Today we have over 400 products that our consultants offer. All of them are exclusive to our consultants. We have designed them. We have tested them for long-term photo storage. We stand behind what we offer with a manufacturer-backed guarantee.

As our parent company, The Antioch Company, seeks to maintain and revitalize seasoned retail business, like Webway, and seeks out new business ventures in hopes of finding another Creative Memories–like success story, we are committed to protecting the relationship our consultants have with their customers. The Antioch Company is also committed to protecting the relationship. Although more than 70 percent of The Creative Memories Collection is manufactured by operating units of The Antioch Company—including the albums, album pages, stickers, papers, and other decorative enhancements—these products are not available for other business units of The Antioch Company. Creative Memories protects the product distinction and price parity in order to protect our consultants' businesses. To offer The Creative Memories Collection in retail stores or through other channels would jeopardize our consultants.

HIGH-TECH FOR THE SAKE OF HIGH-TOUCH

Times have changed. I am in awe of the number of kids who have cell phones. I am amazed that I can send an e-mail to a friend in Australia, and she'll get it almost instantly. These new phones that transmit pictures—how interesting is that?

We continue to advance technologically at amazing rates. And many of these advancements are designed with sharing and communication in mind. Technology is supposed to enhance relationships. We recognize that and want to do what we can to incorporate it into our program where it makes the most sense.

As we protect the relationship between ourselves and our consultants and our consultants and their customers, we must not lose sight of personal interaction.

Sure, we could take orders over the Internet. Sure, we could send out e-mail blasts to large groups of people in a fraction of a second. Sure, we could complete most business transactions without leaving our homes. While all of these actions should be done for convenience sake, they really should be done to open opportunities—to open time—for more quality interaction.

For us, technology should never take the place of human interaction, of that one-on-one service and support. For example, in Chapter 7 we talked about our contact management software BusinessMate that is available for our consultants. This software helps our leaders fulfill their responsibility of training, supporting, and recognizing their downline. The technology—the high-tech software—allows our leaders to quickly sort and filter information about their team's ordering and recruiting activity. By quickly gathering this information, they are able to focus on the high-touch aspects of leadership: the recognition phone calls, congratulations e-mails, gentle order reminders, and development of training topics for their next team meeting.

The lesson here is that high-tech does not replace high-touch. It makes high-touch easier by reducing some of the legwork needed to prepare. High-tech should create more time for high-touch.

MAKE THE CONNECTION

Our consultants have customer contact every day to strengthen and build their relationships. Consultant contact with home office staff is also essential to our success in protecting the relationship. We make every effort to get our employee-owners in contact with our consultants. Anytime we can put a face to the people we are serving, and a face to the people providing the service, we are building and strengthening relationships. We are no longer just a voice on the end of a phone line or a name at the end of an e-mail message. We are Steve in consultant services or Lynette on the picking line. We are Consultant Rosa from North Dakota. We are people who care about each other.

In 1996 at our national convention, Showcase, we had about 2,000 consultants come to St. Cloud, Minnesota, for training and recognition. We invited everyone from manufacturing, distribution, and the office who wasn't working at the event to come and watch the closing ceremonies—the awards show. We felt it was important for the employee-owners to see the passion and commitment our consultants have for what they do. We wanted them to witness first-hand the pride and joy that comes from being a consultant and being a home-based business owner.

The awards show is always a formal event. The amount of sequins, bright lights, and applause rivals any nationally televised awards show.

This particular year, our employee-owners were asked to sit on the second-level catwalk that lines the perimeter and overlooked the auditorium because we didn't have enough seating for them on the main floor.

During final comments at the awards ceremony, Cofounder Rhonda Anderson introduced the people who make the albums, ship the products, and support the consultants' day-to-day business activities. The crowd erupted and jumped to their feet.

For more than 10 minutes, our consultants gave our employee-owners the most enthusiastic and appreciative standing ovation I have ever witnessed. Our staff cried. And I don't think any of them were fully aware of the impact each of them has on our mission. It doesn't matter if they are the people who apply the reinforced edges to the album pages, the shrink wrap to the outside of the packaging, or the labels on the shipping cartons. Each of them has an important role in getting a completed keepsake album in the hands of someone around the world. And that completed album contains the stories, the values, the life lessons that help identify, strengthen, and celebrate the important moments in life. Even though our employee-owners don't actually put the pictures and documentation on the customer's album page, their commitment to product quality and fulfillment makes those priceless gifts a reality. I get goose bumps to this day just thinking about it.

Anytime we have an event, we do our best to get these two groups to meet. We are mutually interdependent, and the more we can do to work together, the better we all will be.

This relationship building hasn't always been easy for our employees. Our consultants love to take pictures. And when we have 5,000 consultants tour our home office and facilities each year, they take a lot of pictures. They photograph all the machines, all the people, even the tour guide who is taking the hour to show them around.

When this first started happening, our employees expressed frustration about feeling like fish in a fishbowl. After we explained that our consultants love to meet and thank the people who help them fulfill the mission, our employees started to understand just how important their role is to the consultants.

They began to realize that they weren't just someone who adds the stitches to our album pages. They weren't just someone who adds shrink wrap to the product. They weren't just someone who keys in numbers day after day after day. Each of them has an essential role in helping get a safe, meaningful keepsake album in someone's hands. And that album will provide the joy, comfort, and sense of belonging to future generations. All employees are part of something so much bigger than themselves. And the work they do today will have far-reaching effects for decades to come.

I don't think they realize the heroes that they truly are.

We are part of something that will change the world one completed photo album at a time. The interface between our consultants and our employees at events and in our work will help ensure sustainability in the future. Our employees are stewards of the company assets. They see the future. They have vision. They are proud of where we are going. And they are committed to getting us there. The synergy of our employees' and consultants' passion is invaluable.

WHAT CAN YOU DO?

As I said before, all businesses are relationship businesses and whatever we can do to protect the relationships we have made and relationships yet to be we must do.

According to Susan McCray of Yankelovich, Inc., an international firm that studies consumer attitudes and forecasts consumer lifestyle and behaviors, consumer attitudes affecting their purchasing decisions have changed dramatically in this millennium.

The Yankelovich MONITOR report shows that 66 percent of consumers feel that businesses will take advantage of the public if the opportunity arises and it is not likely the company will be caught. This is up from 54 percent in 1993.

McCray adds that consumers said they make their buying decisions based on the following:

- If they are treated with respect: 70 percent
- If they feel they are under no pressure to buy: 65 percent
- If they believe the returns policy and process is fair: 61 percent
- If they feel they receive outstanding service: 58 percent

Offering the best-quality product and service is essential. Standing behind products and services is a must. Showing that you care about consumers and fulfilling their needs shows you aren't just out to make a sale (although that is a byproduct of your relationship). All of these things reinforce that you care about your customers and appreciate their business. Meeting or beating competitors' pricing for the same products or services helps you acquire customers, but it isn't necessarily what will keep customers coming back. Building the relationship and protecting it will.

Get employees involved with customers beyond the transaction. Have them send thank you notes and reinforce that they can be reached with questions, comments, or concerns. Have them person alize their interactions. This can be as simple as thanking someone by name. Or, if you have the ability to capture customer preferences—like a favorite product, a favorite table at a restaurant, a particular habit (like one ice cube in your Merlot)—and you can deliver on that without making the customer repeat the information, you protect the relationship.

Whatever you choose to do, make sure your customers feel valued and treated the best. Protect the relationships you have formed.

CHAPTER 10

RESPECT PERSONAL CHOICES

❦

We are responsible for offering rewarding Career Opportunities, incentives, and an invaluable mission for those who choose to embrace them.

We welcome all levels of business activity.

We respect personal choices in life and in business.

And, we do not dictate lifestyles in compensation, incentives, and rewards.

Baby boomers. Generation X. Echo boomers. They make up our population, and each group—and everyone within those groups for that matter—has different attitudes, beliefs, and needs to be met. And they are equally important as a buying public. Diversification doesn't stop with this birth order.

The traditional nuclear family is anything but traditional. And religion and culture from every continent gather together to exist peacefully (the ideal, not always the real) within the confines of one border.

With the changing faces, hearts, and minds of our society, we cannot afford to be exclusive within markets we are trying to reach. All consumers have basic needs that we need to fulfill. One of those needs is to be respected. Does that mean we, as organizations, can be all things to all people? As I said before, not a chance. For example, income levels can clearly define who is in a market, such as if a consumer is part of the new Porsche market or the used Ford market. However, we must be mindful and respectful of our changing environment and adapt accordingly. All people need to be treated with dignity and respect. Their personal choices are simply that, personal choices.

At Creative Memories, we offer rewarding careers, an invaluable mission, and incentives and programs to inspire and motivate. We offer these opportunities to everyone, and people can choose to participate. We recognize that not everyone will choose to do so. Moreover, those who do choose to participate will do so on their own terms. Creative Memories respects their personal choices.

CAREER CHOICES

Creative Memories consultants are offered a rewarding career opportunity. As mentioned before, rewarding can have different meanings for different people. For some, rewarding is the opportunity to make a difference in someone's life by helping capture precious stories in keepsake albums. For others, rewarding is earning a six-figure income while still being able to home school the kids. Whichever area of the spectrum our consultants choose to be a part of, we respect that choice. Their choices, however, impact the compensation they receive.

For the album enthusiast who loves to occasionally share Creative Memories with family and friends or the creative genius who loves to spend 2 hours decorating an album page with stickers and papers, we offer a universal discount on products that they order. When it comes to compensation, their choice is to enjoy the album-making benefits.

The consultants who choose to build a career with Creative Memories are rewarded with commissions, bonuses, and rebates for their business activities.

Creative Memories welcomes all levels of business activity. We understand many of our consultants choose to be with us for our mission. We understand that some enjoy having a full-time career with Creative Memories. And we understand that some may choose to stop being consultants because it isn't the right time in their lives for it. We respect these choices. We offer our opportunities to everyone, regardless of their activity level, and reward accordingly however consultants choose to participate.

Some consultants may even choose to become a leader in our sales force. Approximately 5 percent of our consultants have taken this step. The first level of leadership in our career opportunity is that of the unit leader. Once consultants attain that level by welcoming a minimum of six new people to their team, they stand at a pivotal moment in their career with Creative Memories.

Through their personal business, they continue to share Creative Memories' rewarding opportunities with everyone they meet. Customers, coordinators, and potential new consultants are grateful for the time our leaders take to show the amazing impact Creative Memories will have on their lives.

As leaders, they have an amazing team that looks to them for training, support, and recognition. They serve as a role model. They offer words of encouragement. And they provide direction and vision.

It's an exciting time. It's a rewarding time. And, for some, it can also be a confusing and overwhelming time.

The excitement comes from realizing a goal, from building a business, and from seeing consultants on their teams grow and develop too.

The rewards are many. Financially they receive increased commissions for personal and team efforts. They receive bonuses for training and development of their team. And they receive a monthly expense allowance to help offset the costs of training. Professionally, they are rewarded as they help their team achieve its goals, build their team, and become leaders in their own right. And, personally, they are rewarded by the relationships they build along the way.

This can be a confusing and overwhelming time. Too often, once consultants reach the unit leader level, they are confused about where to invest their time and energy—their personal business of selling and recruiting or their leadership business of training and development of new team members.

For some, they simply stop growing. They have welcomed six new consultants to their team, and they stop recruiting new members to their team. While it is great that they have recruited the minimum number of team members to reach a leadership level, the reality is that you can't stop at six. Any member of a consultant's team may choose to leave the business for whatever reason, so the team needs to be continually growing, or a consultant's business and income could decrease.

These are very real and very common situations, and at this pivotal time, our consultants may choose to continue to grow as a leader or to embrace being a consultant only. We support them in whatever decision they determine is right for them, but we still help cast that vision for what leadership could be. We offer testimonials from other leaders, so our consultants can see the positive impacts (financially, personally, professionally) of making Creative Memories a full-time career.

The reality is that regardless of what leadership level our consultants attain throughout their Creative Memories career, they always will have a personal business and leadership business. This will not change. They must choose, however, where they feel their time is best spent. That choice will vary from leader to leader.

The personal business is what they do best. They teach Home Classes and offer opportunities. This will ensure that they are always in touch with Creative Memories' product and program. This will ensure they have a constant stream of new customers and potential new consultants to build and strengthen their business.

This will ensure their business maintains forward momentum. Because we all know that we have three options in life and in business: we are moving forward, standing still, or falling behind. We want to move forward.

By doing what they do best in their personal business, they will do their best as a leader, too. If that is the path they choose. They will know firsthand what it is like when a Home Class (or "party") cancels or a potential new consultant waits 5 months to join the team. They will know firsthand the importance of goal setting and taking action steps to reach that goal. And they will know firsthand that sometimes you simply need to move on to keep momentum going.

This firsthand experience allows our leaders to talk with confidence about owning a business. It provides credibility. And it shows that they empathize with their team. Their experiences in their personal business will help them do their best as a leader. They will be leading by example. In essence, by choosing to invest in their personal business, they are also choosing to invest in their leadership business. They will be getting double mileage out of that one journey.

Sure, leaders have to learn the career opportunity, spend time getting to know what motivates their team, and keep track of their overall team performance. But the best thing they can do for their team is work their personal business alongside of their team and share experiences.

In addition to doing what our consultants do best, leaders have to love to learn. By being a lifelong student, they will ensure continual growth and development. That will help ensure success.

A leader's commitment to attend training sessions and to ask questions of those around them shows a love of learning. Leaders can always use a refresher course on basic sales skills and interview skills. Leaders can also learn more about inspiring and managing a team. Finally, leaders can brush up on business skills like public speaking, bookkeeping, and money management.

Encouraging team members to be lifelong students also shows a love of learning. Again, the lesson here is that we are either moving forward, moving backward, or standing still. Learning provides forward motion.

And, finally, we encourage our leaders and all consultants to keep their businesses simple. It is a wonderful challenge to be a leader. But one has to have balance and priorities. Leaders don't reinvent the wheel on training. They don't share 1,001 good ideas that overwhelm. Leaders choose to stick to the basics.

Leadership is rewarding, and it is attained because of persistence, commitment, and vision. It is not necessarily for everybody. Less than 5 percent of our consultants choose to commit to leadership. Leadership is truly a matter of choice. Creative Memories respects a consultant's choice to be a leader. Creative Memories also respects a consultant's choice to be an album enthusiast. We do not push or coerce people to be a leader. We simply offer the opportunity, and let consultants make the choice to participate.

Personal choice impacts us each day whether we work in a direct-selling environment, education, retail, the corporate world, etc. Anyone who manages a team or is in human resources can vouch for this. And personal choice will impact work performance, compensation, and work ethic.

Go for the Gold

I remember FloJo at the 1988 Olympic Games in Seoul. I remember her long flowing hair, her flashy one-legged clothes, and her vibrant red, white, blue, and gold nails. I don't remember her looking overwhelmed.

She earned the title World's Fastest Woman that year by setting records in the 100- and 200-meter dashes. Those records earned her two of the three gold medals she won.

What always amazes me about Olympic athletes is how easy they make their sport look. You know they train hard for years. You know they adjust their lifestyle—their food, their rest, their schedule—to maximize their performance. And, as in FloJo's case, they make those 10.49 seconds of sprinting seem effortless. They float. They fly.

Business performance should be the same. The best business athletes accomplish amazing feats without the angst. I've told more than one of our team members that I appreciate the work they are doing and the quality of work they are doing; they simply need to make it look easier. They need to go for the gold. They should receive attention for their results and not because they came in on a Saturday to get their work done. Our COO, Asha Morgan Moran, summed it up this way, "You don't get brownie points for angst. You get it for the deliverables."

Personal choice will impact the time and effort that employees put into their work and their level of growth and development. As leaders, we need to recognize those choices and compensate accordingly with accolades, special projects, responsibility, and/or benefits.

Each year, usually around September when wage increases are awarded throughout the home office and our facilities, we will hear some recurring discussions about why someone should have a larger increase in compensation. For one person, it could be that they are at work until 7 p.m. every night trying to get caught up when everyone else walks out the door at 4:30. For another, it could be because they took a cut in pay to join our team. For another, it could be that they have been with us for more than 10 years, and that longevity should count for something.

The reality is, these employees made personal choices to not get work done within 45 hours each week. That could be due to procrastination, poor project management, too much tweaking of projects, an inability to ask for help, or any number of reasons. In regards to pay, it is personal choice to accept a position for less pay. And, in regards to longevity, that is rewarded with service anniversary recognition. Longevity is not an indication of job performance. Growth, development, and improved efficiency are. As one of our management team put it, "You've done the same job at the same level for 10 years. So, you've really put in 1 year of improved performance."

As leaders, we should respect these personal choices. It is not our responsibility to make up for whatever employees feel are lacking in their jobs as a result of their choices. However, it is our responsibility to examine our resources, skills, workload, training, and development programs, and our recognition and compensation programs to ensure we are doing what we can to offer the best work environment for our employees. We must act for the good of the whole.

On the Road of Life

At Creative Memories, we are often asked if we are a "Christian company." The answer is we are a values-based company. Our statement of highest purpose, corporate values, and guiding principles allow us to operate in a manner that is welcoming of all beliefs and cultures.

If we consider for a moment that our mission is to help others preserve the defining moments and attributes of their lives, faith is a large part of how people define themselves. To limit our mission and our reach to those who recognize and worship God (whether they be Baptists, Catholics, Jews, Lutherans, etc.) is to discredit the other millions of individuals who live morally sound, beautiful lives. They simply choose to have faith in Allah or Buddha or nature or something else. This brings them comfort. This helps define who they are. Their beliefs should be captured and celebrated, so future generations can learn the faith that guided their family.

And being inclusive does not stop with religion. We must welcome the modern family. That family could be the traditional nuclear family. In some cases, family could mean a group of individuals who choose to live together under one roof and love and cherish each other.

The sitcom *Kate and Allie*, which ran on CBS from 1984 to 1989, celebrated the varying definition of family two decades ago. Kate and Allie were divorcees who found comfort supporting each other as single parents living in the same household.

We must be welcoming of culture. That, too, defines who we are and should be captured and celebrated. According to the July 1, 2002, U.S. Census Bureau data, almost 200 million people in the United States consider themselves white. More than 38 million consider themselves to be Hispanic or Latino. More than 36 million consider themselves black or African American. More than 12 million consider themselves to be Asian or Asian American. And more than 3.5 million consider themselves to be Native American Indian or Alaskan Indian. With this rich, cultural population, businesses, schools, and government cannot afford to simply think, advertise, and operate with a "white" focus. We, as a society, have so much to learn and celebrate.

Is it easy to be inclusive? Well, it can be a change in mindset. We need to learn about lifestyles and beliefs that may be different from our own. We need to seek out ways of life that may not be part of our everyday exposure. We need to do all we can to learn those differences and incorporate them into our product, program, and promotional materials.

Creative Memories is based in central Minnesota. The population is predominantly white. Catholics and Lutherans are the predominant religious groups. How do we, at Creative Memories, learn about life outside our geographic region? We take to the streets in focus groups or conduct surveys to learn about a wide range of religions and cultures and how these unfold on keepsake album pages.

We facilitate discussions that seek to understand. Sometimes, people are afraid to ask questions about culture or religion because they do not want to appear ignorant. My argument would be that if you are willing to ask and willing to learn, this shows you are open minded. And those being asked should be appreciative and respectful to have the opportunity to educate others about the beliefs and traditions that are important to them.

When being respectful of lifestyle choices, we look beyond culture, race, and religion, as well. When Creative Memories first started out, many of our promotional materials included tall blonde folks. And our winter promotional pieces usually included snow. Much of the United States is not populated with blondes, nor do many of the states even see snow. We made a common mistake of creating an image that was familiar to us, what was in our own backyard. Unfortunately, this demonstrated that we were not aware of life outside Stearns County, and we had to change.

Our domestic promotional materials now reflect the diverse population of the United States and the diverse landscape. And, although they are now diverse, the images we use here are not necessarily appropriate for our international markets. Those markets have their own set of images and traditions that are appropriate for them.

At Creative Memories, we strive to represent inclusiveness in our interaction with consultants and in our consultants' interactions with their customers. Beyond the images and faces that represent Creative Memories on stage, in print, and on the Web, our word choices also must be inclusive. Therefore, when we thank a consultant's support network—those who encourage them in their career—we make every effort to acknowledge that this may be a spouse, a family member, or a dear friend. Not everyone has a supportive husband. Not everyone has a husband. (Herein lies another one of our attempts to be inclusive. Of our 90,000 consultants, we have approximately 150 men. The female pronoun is our typical point of reference; however, we try to remain inclusive of both genders in written word and speech.)

We also recognize that consultants may want to thank a higher power for the blessings they have in their lives. We encourage them to express their gratitude; however, their thanks cannot be imposing their viewpoint on others. For example, we are quite comfortable with someone saying in a speech, "I thank God every day for the blessings in my life." We are not comfortable with someone saying in a speech, "You should thank God every day for the blessings in your life." Why? That phrasing imposes another's belief on others.

With our ever-changing society, we cannot afford to be exclusive or intolerant of others. We must be inclusive and respectful of other religious beliefs, cultural traditions, lifestyles, and even those who choose to live without snow.

STAYING CLEAR OF THE GOLDEN HANDCUFFS

The final part of this guiding principle is that Creative Memories does not dictate lifestyles in compensation, incentives, and rewards. We recognize that some companies offer cars, mortgage payments, and fur coats as rewards for business achievement. While we respect this decision and understand it is a recognizable part of the cultures of these companies, we choose not to offer these types of lifestyle rewards. I will admit it was not an easy decision (and we do hear about it occasionally); however, it is the right decision for us.

We never want to be put into a position where we would embarrass our consultants. Because our business of direct selling is one that consultants can choose to participate in on their own terms, we do see businesses grow, falter, and fluctuate with the changing needs of consultants' personal priorities. And the risk of having a consultant lose a house or have a car repossessed because that consultant is no longer meeting the minimum requirements to receive those rewards is too great for the temporary satisfaction of giving the reward. We also never want to make our consultants feel uncomfortable because an award is not a reflection of their lifestyle choices.

We provide financial incentives through cash bonuses, rebates, and commissions. Consultants earn for their personal and team activity. Consultants choose to earn these by conducting business activities that meet minimum requirements. If our consultants make the personal choice to alter their lifestyle with the money that they earn, that is their choice. If they want to build a dream home, they can. If they want to use the money to provide scholarships for children in their community, they can. And if they want to finance mission work in other countries, they can. It is their choice to invest the money they earn in ways that are appropriate for their personal beliefs, wants, and needs. We respect those choices. We do not want to dictate investments for them or lock them into a lifestyle they may one day not be able to maintain. As Asha puts it, "People have to want to be here. We don't want them here in golden handcuffs."

Creative Memories never wants to be in a position where we could potentially impose a lifestyle on anyone. We want our consultants to be comfortable with the rewards they receive for their achievements. If we provide financial rewards, consultants and their families can invest those funds into their lifestyles as they see fit.

The lesson in this guiding principle is that businesses need to be respectful of personal choices. Personal choices can represent whether or not a consumer chooses to take part in your organization's product or service. Pilots for an airline that I fly regularly often say at the end of the flight, "We recognize that you have choices in your travel, and we thank you for choosing us."

Personal choices can be a commitment to work. Personal choices can represent the way in which people choose to live. In business, we need to be respectful of these choices as we welcome and support our consumers and our employees.

CHAPTER 11

GO FOR THE GOOD
OF THE WHOLE

~⚬————⚬~

Creative Memories is responsible for making decisions
that do the greatest good for the greatest number of
Consultants, employee-owners, and the communities
(in that order) in which we operate.

We know that we cannot be all things to all people, so it is our responsibility to do the best we can to support the greatest number.

Consider for a moment that you ask your family what they would like to have for dinner. Your spouse wants steak and potatoes. The 5-year-old wants chicken nuggets and macaroni and cheese (that's always a given), and the teenagers want pizza. You'd be happy with a salad. What do you do?

Obviously you can't make it all. Your goal should be to make a well-balanced meal that has something for everybody. And you can provide options. Perhaps it is pizza one night, chicken nuggets another, and steak on Saturday.

The point is you can't please everybody, even in a small group.

Now, take that principle and apply it to a field of 90,000 independent business owners. What are the chances that you will get several thousand of these business owners to agree on any one thing at any one time and still maintain company sustainability? In the direct-selling industry, members of the independent sales force are pretty passionate about their product line, the program they offer, and their own home-based business. Something as simple as discontinuing a photo album color can create quite a stir. Such was the case with the Save the Teals campaign.

Teal was an album color in our line for many years. As a trend color, it was popular for a while. Eventually, it lost its popularity, and, without a doubt, became one of our lowest sellers. While other albums were purchased by the tens and hundreds of thousands each year, the teal album was lucky to break a few thousand. While it lived a good life, it was time to say goodbye to it. As a result, we decided to discontinue it. And we positioned it as an opportunity to open up space for a new product in The Creative Memories Collection. Now, in order to protect the relationship, we gave our consultants several months warning, so they could contact their customers and let them know of the change. We wanted those who had an entire album collection comprised of teal albums to get more of the albums in hand before the color was discontinued. We didn't want them to suddenly, unexpectedly be at a loss for the album color of their choice.

As expected, once we announced the teal album would be discontinued, the album gained in popularity. Everybody wanted it. And some very passionate consultants weren't happy with our decision to discontinue the color. Thus, a Save the Teals campaign ensued, and the home office was flooded with voice mails and e-mails requesting to keep that color in our line.

We appreciated the love and commitment people had for this album, but the choice had been made, and it was the best decision for our consultants as a whole. By removing the teal album, it was one less album our consultants had to inventory, especially since it was a low seller. Removing the teal album also opened up opportunities for newer product to be introduced. We didn't simply want to keep introducing new product; that would be too much for our consultants to try and manage. And the resources invested in producing that album could be redirected to a more popular product.

Following our guiding principles, we made sure we communicated clearly and concisely why it was being discontinued. We protected the relationship the consultants have with their customers by giving them a long lead time to contact their customers who had a collection of teal albums. And we didn't knee-jerk react to the protest by deciding to keep the album in our line—Don't knee jerk is another principle which you'll read about in Chapter 12.

The hoopla eventually faded, and we made it through.

Decision making is not always easy. And, ultimately, some people will be upset about the decision. Because the members of our volunteer sales force can come and go as they please, it is in our best interest to make the best decisions that provide the greatest good for the greatest number of consultants.

When we joined the Direct Selling Association in the late 1980s, we met Alan Luce, President of Luce and Associates. At the time, Alan had been in the industry for over 20 years, and he was readily available to answer any questions we had as a start-up company in the direct-selling industry. He showed us the ropes, so to speak.

He now has his own consulting firm to offer advice to new and established direct-selling companies, and one of the key messages he imparts in his Learning the Ropes seminar is that companies have to make decisions that are for the good of the whole organization.

In his seminar, Alan teaches four questions that help companies decide if their decisions are in the best interest of the overall organization. While these questions were designed for the direct-selling industry, they have application in general business as well.

Before we get to the four questions, we should revisit some general ideas about the psychographics of direct sellers. They are an independent volunteer sales force. As with all volunteers, if they for any reason become unhappy with us or our products and programs or believe they are being mistreated, they simply don't place another order. They simply stop being a part of our organization.

This business truth applies to all types of customers. They can choose to invest time, money, and energy into whichever products or services they feel best about. They may love a brand, the quality, a price point, convenience, but if they ever lose faith in the company they are doing business with, they will seek products or services elsewhere.

Let me give you an example. A girlfriend of mine went to buy a sport utility vehicle recently. She knew what she wanted in terms of the bells and whistles. She knew the price she was willing to pay. And she was in a position to get the vehicle of her choice on the spot. She brought her husband along for fun; she figured he'd enjoy test driving the SUV.

When they arrived at the dealership, the salesperson who greeted them shook her husband's hand. And, throughout their 2 hours there, he talked only to her husband about what *he* was looking for. Even though my friend kept answering the questions and was the one who would be paying for the vehicle, the salesperson continued to focus on the husband.

Out of frustration my friend chose to leave that night without the SUV. She did go back a few days later planning to purchase it, though, after she calmed down a bit. The same salesperson asked her why she didn't bring her husband along. She informed the salesperson that she was the one buying the vehicle and since he had been so disrespectful toward her that she chose to do business elsewhere. And she did.

She has not been back, and she tells anyone who inquires about her vehicle not to shop at this particular dealership because of her experience.

Right or wrong, this is the power that consumers have. If they have any reason to be disenchanted with an organization, their word-of-mouth criticisms can have devastating effects. Customers are not obligated to do business with you. They make the choice on a voluntary basis.

Now that we have a clear understanding of how our salespeople, as well as our customers, think and feel, we can focus on Alan's four questions to determine if something is good for the organization. The four questions should be asked in the following order based on how large each group is and how much is at stake with each group, that is, based on how vulnerable we are, as an organization, to this group.

1. *Is this decision a good one for the new and part-time salespeople? Why?*
   - Does it add to or reduce their profit?
   - Does it add to or reduce their paperwork?
   - Does it make placing orders easier?
   - Does it make recruiting and sponsoring easier?
   - Does it make becoming a salesperson easier or harder?
   - Does it make it easier or harder to sell the product?

   If a decision impacts any of these areas negatively, the company should not do it.

   New and part-time salespeople make up 80 percent of our sales force. As a company, we cannot afford to lose them. Individually, they do not make up large sales volumes. In fact, they may account for only $500 every 3 months. Collectively, they are quite a force. The 13,000 of them who wait until the last few days of the month to place their minimum order requirement account for almost $6.5 million in sales that month. Beyond the dollars they generate, this group of consultants has tremendous reach if they are happy or dissatisfied with Creative Memories for any reason. The word-of-mouth impact they could have on the organization is staggering. Just think back to the example of my friend with the SUV. She told everyone she knew of the negative experience she had with a local car dealer. She probably convinced others to not shop there as well.

   On the flip side, more than 68 percent of those who choose to be a part of Creative Memories learned of us through a friend or family member who had had a positive experience. This statistic reinforces the power of a positive word-of-mouth endorsement. The consultants that make up 80 percent of our sales force are just like their customers. And they should be. Almost every consultant we have started out as a Creative Memories customer or coordinator for a Home Class. This is typical in the direct-selling industry.

   "Most direct-selling salespeople joined the business because they love the products and purchase them for their own use," says Alan.

"They were customers first, buying the products because they believe they represent good value for the money. If they believe that a product is priced too high (they wouldn't pay that much for it!), they won't sell it. If they believe that a product doesn't perform well, they won't sell it. Their mindset is more in tune with their customers than it is with the company marketing department."

You want to keep the largest segment of your customer base happy. To do this, think like a customer in your decision making and implement what does the greatest good for the greatest number.

2. *Is this decision good for the new and midlevel sales leaders who are trying to build a full-time business? Why?* At the first levels of leadership—our unit leaders and senior unit leaders—our consultants are trying to strike a balance between their personal business activity (their own personal selling and recruiting) and their team's activity. As leaders, they are responsible for training, supporting, and recognizing their downline (i.e., the people on their team).

Any decision we make that impacts this group must make their jobs easier. If a decision will make their job harder, we shouldn't do it.

Why? Our leaders are responsible for building strong, sustainable teams. They develop the leaders of tomorrow. If the leadership role is not attractive, if it is not rewarding, the field won't grow. I'm sure you've all heard it said that 20 percent of the people are responsible for 80 percent of the work. While the percentages don't match completely, the similar is true in direct selling. Less than 5 percent of our field holds leadership positions. Yet their teams are responsible for millions of dollars each year and thousands of new consultants joining Creative Memories each year.

We must not hurt their ability to lead and grow. So we continually evaluate our compensation plan to ensure it rewards the midlevel leaders for their personal and leadership activity. We create products and programs that help streamline their leadership responsibility, so it is easier to fulfill their leadership role while maintaining their personal business. The BusinessMate software we talked about with the "Make it easy" guiding principle is a perfect example of this. We also provide standardized recognition programs that define sales and recruiting achievement levels and a catalog of awards for meeting those levels that leaders can order to recognize their teams. And we provide unit meeting outlines for them to use as they host their monthly training meetings with their teams.

Anything we can do to make this transition from consultant to leader easier and rewarding is important. These new leaders could eventually become the leaders of multimillion dollar teams in our sales force.

3. *Is this decision a good one for the top level of sales leaders in the compensation plan?* According to Alan, "Decisions that only impact the top salespeople are not as black and white as the two categories set out above. The very top salespeople have begun to move out of 'volunteer status,'" he says. "All or a substantial portion of the family income comes out of their direct-selling business. As a group they have begun to think more like businesspeople and less like customers. So, for instance, if a company action would be good for the new and part-time folks, good for new and midlevel sales leaders, and a bit frustrating for top sales leaders, it may be worth making the decision and taking the action."

Does this mean that top-level leaders are less important? No, it does not. Top-level leaders have a lot at stake in their business. But because of the size of their home-based business, they recognize and understand the complexities of large business ownership. They understand that not all business decisions are easy, but decisions must be made that impact the entire organization. On another note, because of the relationship top-level leaders have formed with the corporate office throughout their business development, the dialogue tends to be more candid as we work together to plan and implement new programs. Major initiatives are not implemented without feedback from the top-level leaders. And seeking this feedback can sometimes be a painful process, but it is essential to the success of the initiative and relationship between the home office and the field.

4. *Is this decision good for the company?* The company is always last in this question-and-answer process. Why? Ultimately, what is good for the sales force should be good for the company. If consultants can operate their businesses efficiently and effectively, be proud of their product and program, and be honored to share the career opportunity, then sales and recruiting growth should follow. The converse is not always true. What is good for the company may not be good for the sales force.

Every so often, direct-selling companies will consider offering their products through retail stores in hopes of building brand awareness and generating new leads. Some may do this in a kiosk at a mall or in a department store. Others may put their product and brand name right on the store shelves next to products of a similar nature. While this retail adventure will generate sales for the organization, it literally kills the consultant business as consumers seek to purchase products through the retail channel rather than the direct-selling channel. If we consider the four questions asked above, this decision was initially good for the company's bottom line but not for any level of the sales force. That, ultimately, hurt the relationship between the consultants and the company.

"By forcing ourselves to view each decision from the perspective of the decision's potential impact on the sales force, we can avoid a lot of dumb mistakes," Alan says. "By definition, any action that adversely impacts the sales force and leaders is not a good decision for the company."

If the answer to all four questions is positive, the company should proceed with the decision.

We can apply these questions to events in our history. Each winter, we host regional conventions throughout North America. We visit as many as 22 cities in a 4-week period and reach as many as 18,000 of our consultants. Regional conventions are a time to educate, motivate, and celebrate. For newer consultants, it also may be their first introduction to a corporate-sponsored event.

Picking regional convention locations is an easy decision for us. We seek out cities that will draw the greatest number of consultants to the event. A computer software program that we use identifies where the largest concentrations of our consultants are, and the software maps out consultants within a few hours of that key area. Sometimes, moving our convention to a city a few hours north, east, or west of its previous location will allow us to draw several hundred more consultants.

While Creative Memories has a sound business reason for wanting to draw more consultants to our events, communicating a change of venue is not always received highly. The consultants who previously only had to drive 30 minutes or so to an event and could stay at their house rather than a hotel are upset because of the added expense and inconvenience to them. From a business perspective, though, the more consultants we can get together to network, celebrate accomplishments, and train, the better we all are as an organization. Even those people who were upset by our decision benefited by being able to reach a broader network of consultants. The enthusiasm and education shared is contagious, and sales and recruiting numbers will reflect that following an event. In other words, this decision allowed us to go for the good of the whole.

TO GIVE AND DO GOOD

Organizations and people who are profitable and have financial resources are expected to share their wealth and help those organizations and people who are less fortunate. Unfortunately, the number of needy organizations and individuals faced with growing demands and fewer financial resources is staggering. This expectation presents the challenge that most organizations face: how much to give and to whom. This challenge is addressed in the principle, Go for the good of the whole.

Currently, Creative Memories receives 10 to 20 requests a day from people seeking out funds or donations of products for very worthy causes. Someone I met who works for a national retailer told me they receive over 200 requests a day. And when these calls and letters arrive, the person requesting the donation has a heart-wrenching story to share. We learn of the number of people impacted by a devastating disease. We hear of the heartbreak from families who lose everything in a natural or human-made disaster. We hear of the less-fortunate populations in our community who have no money, no homes, no education, no resources to make a better life for themselves.

All of these causes are important. All of these causes are worthwhile. All of these causes need additional resources for research, education, and outreach. All of these organizations cannot be funded out of one company's pocketbook. This is one of the most painful areas to make decisions in the interest of the good of the whole. We want to strengthen the communities in which we are a part. We also want to be a good corporate citizen that our consultants and employees are proud of. By picking and choosing which organizations to support with donations, we try to do the greatest good for the greatest numbers. By making a decision, however, we have to turn others away. Because many of our requests come to us via an employee or a consultant, we have to make sure we communicate the reasons for our decisions clearly and concisely in order to protect the relationship—the pride—our consultants and employees have for our organization. Our charitable giving is one business activity that is directed by many of our guiding principles.

TO STRENGTHEN AND PROTECT

Donations requests we receive fall into one of two categories: a request for product or a request for funds.

From a product donation standpoint, Creative Memories is often called upon to donate albums and album-making supplies because our mission is perfectly aligned with a cause. A completed album could bring hope to foster children who may lack a sense of identity, families coping with a tragic illness, families who lost a lifetime of pictures to a natural disaster. The reality is, though, that if we donate products to the general public we would bypass our consultants and potentially damage their business and their trust in us as an organization. If we were a retail store, it would be easier to donate product and track the expense that comes with the donation. We cannot quantify the potential impact on our consultants. Having the company donate products to the general public is not in the best interest of our consultants. Instead, we encourage those who request product donations from us to get in touch with a local Creative Memories consultant. Our consultants may be able to assist with a donation of product or a fund-raising activity or even the instruction to help others complete a keepsake album in a time that may be difficult. Particularly in instances where families are coping with tragedy, the personal assistance of a consultant is invaluable.

From a financial standpoint, no organization can donate money to every request that comes in. So organizations must define what they are aligning themselves with in order to prioritize and fulfill donation requests.

One organization I know of donates to causes that help children. This broad umbrella could include literacy programs, cancer research, foster care, and after-school programs. They have not aligned themselves with one particular organization as much as they have aligned themselves with helping children.

Another organization I know of donates to causes that help end domestic violence. These donations could go to care facilities, community awareness projects, or education programs. But all donations focus on ending domestic violence.

Some organizations choose to align themselves with one organization, like the American Cancer Society.

Creative Memories has aligned itself with the Alzheimer's Association over the last few years to help find a cure for memory loss. Our mission and program is geared toward helping others preserve the stories and memories that define who they are. By completing keepsake albums, people gain a sense of identity, a sense of belonging, and a sense of history. Keepsake albums help people recognize all that is good about life, particularly in difficult times. Albums also provide hope for current and future generations. The Alzheimer's Association is committed to finding a cure and providing hope for those afflicted with this disease that robs people of their memories and their sense of identity. Common things that most of us take for granted, like the names of our loved ones or directions home, can be lost for patients with Alzheimer's disease. Our mission and that of the Alzheimer's Association mirror each other.

Since 2002, the Creative Memories home office and our consultants have teamed up to raise funds for the Alzheimer's Association. The first year of our partnership, we raised over $1 million for research and education. Funds were raised through the sales of an exclusive photo album called the Triumph Album. Our Time for Triumph campaign also included corporate sponsorship of the annual Memory Walks hosted by local chapters of the association. And, finally, our consultants rallied walk teams to raise money through sponsorships.

While our partnership with the Alzheimer's Association benefited the national organization as well as local chapters, some companies choose to only participate in local requests that are brought to the company from an employee. Others reach out regionally and nationally. Others, still, focus on the adage: Feed a man a fish, and he eats for a day. Teach him to fish, and he eats for a lifetime. I know of some organizations that only focus on programs that teach and empower others to improve their quality of life. For example, they might donate to a literacy program rather than a homeless shelter because the literacy program would equip participants with a valuable life skill.

Charitable giving and community involvement are areas of decision making that clearly need to be defined in order for an organization to do the greatest good for the greatest number. Yet, even in the spirit of giving and helping others, decisions can be difficult. In the process of doing what is best for everybody, somebody will feel left out and disagree with a decision. We understand that some individuals will be frustrated, some will be passionate about expressing what they feel is the right thing to do, and others, still, may choose to no longer support your business. That is okay. While it is not enjoyable to handle conflict nor is it fun to lose a customer or colleague, it is human nature and the nature of business. Your goal should always be to do what is in the best interest of the greatest number of people.

Before implementing any change, determine what negative impact it could have. Brainstorm all options. Understand that some people might quit. The phones might ring off the hook with frustrated people. Sales may dip. If it doesn't work, we get "egg on our face" and have to change again. Determine what the worst-case scenario could be as a result of a decision you make, and ask yourself this one question: "Can you live with that?"

If you can live with the potential consequences, proceed. If not, find another option. There's always more than one option to consider. If plan A or B doesn't work, find plan C, D, or E.

Don't paralyze yourself with the *or*—this choice *or* that choice. Find an alternative that provides the greatest good for the greatest number. Doing what is good for the whole will lead you to your greatest success.

CHAPTER 12

DON'T KNEE JERK

❧ ——— ❧

Creative Memories is responsible for doing its
homework before implementing change in
product, program, and policy. Creative Memories
is also responsible for letting changes run their
course before amending them.

In our early years, we looked a lot like a peewee hockey team. You know what I mean—the whole team goes wherever the puck is. There's no zone defense, no clarity of roles and responsibilities. Everyone just runs to where the action is and reacts. On the ice, it can be quite entertaining. It doesn't, however, play well in the business environment.

We learned this lesson early on each time our phone lines would light up with 300 consultants wanting to give commentary on a change in our program. And we always listen to each call and explain our rationale behind the change. We recognize that change can be difficult for many. But change really is the only constant in life and in business. And it is up to us to determine how we manage change for our future success. We cannot remain stagnant.

We are either active or inactive. Both will yield results. They just may not be results one would hope for. However things turn out, we must not be afraid to try and not be paralyzed by the fear of negative opinion. And we have to let change run its course to see if it is effective.

In the early 1990s, we learned the value of holding our ground and letting changes run their course. We implemented a change in our commission structure to allow for greater rewards for building a team. At first, we only paid commissions on consultants' first line (those they recruited directly).

We wanted to reward consultants, though, for training and encouraging their first-line consultants to build teams of their own. One way to facilitate this business-building activity was to offer commissions on second- and third-line consultants as well. So consultants would be rewarded for their consultants' sales as well as their consultants' consultants' sales, up to three levels.

This change would lead to a richer earnings opportunity for consultants who chose to build their teams.

The downside was that in order to fund this change in our career plan, we had to decrease the amount of commission consultants earned from their personal sales, so we could also reward for sales on their second and third lines. While the decrease in commission on personal sales impacted short-term, immediate earnings, it really wasn't a downside, because the exponential growth on their second and third lines would more than make up for the commission on their own personal sales.

We knew, though, that people would only see and react to the part about reducing personal commissions.

We chose to send everyone a letter explaining the change and why the change was made. We also explained the positive impact the change would have on their personal business. Then, we did something unorthodox. We said that nobody could call the home office to discuss this change until 5 days had passed. We wanted everyone to read about the change, get passed their initial emotional reaction, reread the change, absorb it, understand it, and then call us if they needed to.

Very few people called, and I know it is because they were not given the opportunity to simply react. Our consultants had to read the information presented, digest it, think about it for a few days, and formulate their opinion on the matter. When they were asked to stop and think rather than read and react, our consultants could see that this was a win-win change for everyone in the field and at the home office. They didn't knee-jerk react to the change, and we didn't knee-jerk react in response to the field.

Does this mean, then, that we should never reverse a change we have made? Absolutely not. We all make mistakes in life and in business; we're not denying that. We prefer to call them learning experiences, and as long as they are not recurring, they really aren't mistakes. Change is hard. Our immediate reaction when faced with change is to take action. I say stop and hold tight.

RUNNING THEIR COURSE

Our newest career plan, which we introduced in July 1999, offered plenty of opportunity for us to knee jerk.

We felt it would help ensure our sustainability by accomplishing these four things:

- Level off the ordering cycle by rewarding consistency in monthly sales orders
- Reward consistency for the three key business activities of selling, recruiting, and leadership development
- Make the unit leader level (our first level of leadership) more attractive
- Spend the same amount of money as previously, just reallocate it for the good of the whole

Before implementing the career plan, we ran test models to make sure that we did the right thing, that we were offering a new plan that was in the best interest of our field and the long-term viability of the company.

We implemented it in July 1999 and gave a 6-month grace period for consultants to get used to it. We also provided training events and printed more than 1.5 million collateral materials to help understand the changes and to help leaders teach their teams about the new plan. And we hired a temporary call-center staff trained specifically to answer all frequently asked questions, document all concerns, and inform us of any growing trends in our field's perception of the plan.

We knew we would get feedback. Our field was having to relearn an entire plan (how they earned money, what was expected of them, how they reward their hostesses). Everything was new. And people weren't happy about it. It's not that it wasn't a good plan. We had done our homework. It's just that it was new.

Despite the calls expressing frustration, disappointment, alternative options, and the like, we let the field know that we had to let the new career plan run its course—a key part of this guiding principle. We had to watch patterns of business activity and payout to see if we were getting the trends we had hoped for. And on a project like this monitoring trends takes years. It's not something we can gauge overnight, or even in a few months. But we promised to monitor the change and adjust accordingly, if need be.

Four years after that implementation, we have only made minor adjustments. For example, we added more opportunities for sales consistency bonuses because the field sales activity increased, and we want to reward them for that. Overall, the plan has accomplished what we set out to do. Ordering patterns have leveled. Ordering has become more consistent. And, at our leadership levels, annual compensation has increased a minimum of 41 percent. In many cases, it is much higher.

On another note (just to revisit the Communicate clearly and concisely principle), the temporary call-center staff we hired and trained to answer career plan questions was scheduled to be with us for 6 months. As a result of communicating clearly and concisely through our training events and printed materials, we were able to disband the special call center after 2 weeks. The implementation was a huge success for our consultants and our home office team.

The lesson here is simple. All change will inspire a reaction. Let the reaction happen. Just make sure you've done your due diligence. Determine what is in the best interest of the whole (this may be your company, your customers, your community, your employees), brainstorm the worst-case scenario that could result from the change, and implement. Also have an exit strategy. Assume the best, but plan for the worst.

DON'T BE PARALYZED BY FEAR

While the knee-jerk reaction can make an organization look ill-prepared and unsure, inactivity can stifle the company's growth and sustainability. Because people tend to fear the reaction a change may cause, they become paralyzed by fear and do nothing. Although this guiding principle focuses mainly on reacting to change, it also opens up the opportunity to discuss resistance to change for fear of the reaction. Neither case is good for a growing business.

In the 1960s, the Campbell Soup Company was a solidly profitable business. They contributed little effort beyond the existing product line and processes they were used to. A man named Gordon McGovern, who worked in the bakery division of the company, wanted Campbell to do more. Before long, he developed a line of premium cookies, and sales for the company shot sky high. The brand name for these premium cookies was Pepperidge Farm.

When McGovern was named chairman of the company a few years later, he successfully opened new markets again with a line of gourmet soups. What's even more important than his sales success with these ventures is that his take-risk attitude soon permeated the company.

Like Campbell's Soup, Creative Memories knows that although we have experienced a comfortable level of success with the practices we have established through the years, we can't simply rest on our laurels and expect success to continue. We have to work to maintain the levels we have already achieved. And we have to have a vision for what we can be. As Microsoft so poignantly asks in their advertisements, "Where do you want to go today?"

We can't adhere to the old adage "If it ain't broke, don't fix it." We must face risk and implement change. We risk through action, *and* we risk through *in*action. Which will yield better results?

Often, risk seems to carry with it the impressions of being in peril or of exposing ourselves to failure. But risk also carries with it the perception of possibility. And possibility presents opportunities for success and prospects of something new and exciting. Calculated risks carry the likelihood of growth. When we perceive risk as opening up possibility, we wait for opportunity to present itself.

Here is an example of what I mean. When I moved to St. Cloud, Minnesota, to oversee the purchase of the Webway photo album manufacturer, this was a risk because I had never lived more than 15 miles from where I was born. I was planning to leave what I'd always known as home, my family, and my coworkers. But I saw the possibility of turning this album manufacturer around and rebuilding it after bankruptcy.

Because I perceived risk as possibility, I dove into the move and my new responsibilities. The opportunity presented itself when I answered the after-hours phone call from Rhonda Anderson in 1987. And the rest, you know, is history.

Creative Memories was built on the perception of possibility. Was it a risk for Rhonda and I to plan and propose the concept of Creative Memories to our CEO? Absolutely. Was it a risk for our parent company, The Antioch Company, to pursue this business venture in a distribution model we were not familiar with? Absolutely. But when we call it a risk, we perceived it as potential for company growth, potential for helping others preserve their memories, and potential to provide rewarding career opportunities for others. The impressions of peril, threat, or exposure to failure really never crossed our minds. We perceived the possibilities. And look at the positive impact we are now making on the world.

As I said, you will risk through your activity, and you will risk through your inactivity. But which will yield the most promising results for personal and professional development, for business, and for your family's financial well-being?

Take risks and don't be afraid of the reaction. Simply wait it out a little while before you offer your next plan of action.

STAND FIRM, BUT KEEP YOUR FINGERS ON THE PULSE

The big question we often get is, "How do you know when to bend and when to stand strong?" That's a tough one to answer. My first thought would be that change has to be purposeful rather than simply for the sake of change. For example, when we implemented changes to our career plan, both times we had a specific goal in mind. Our first change in the early 1990s was to open additional earning opportunities for our consultants. Our second change, as I mentioned, was to level out the ordering cycle, reward consistency, and attract new leaders. We, as Stephen Covey says in his *The 7 Habits of Highly Effective People*, had the end in mind. The changes to our career plan, then, had to lead us to our desired end result.

In the case of the Campbell Soup Company discussed earlier, its goal was to continue to grow and sustain the organization. Although the company was continually profitable, times change and the company needed to be looking for ways to adapt so it could remain a growing company.

When objectives are clearly defined, due diligence is next. Find a benchmark, something to research and compare to, something to aspire to or surpass. In the case of our career plan, we looked at half a dozen other plans in the direct-selling industry to see what companies were offering. We wanted to see what options were available and determine what our best course of action would be. Our final plan was a unique hybrid that included some of our own ideas as well as elements we liked from other industry leaders.

Once you have done research into what changes might help you meet your objectives, draft a plan. Then shoot holes in it. Run test scenarios of how it could play out. Brainstorm what could go wrong and what exit strategies you have in mind for dealing with backlash. Solicit feedback from employees, customers, and noncustomers to get their concerns, blessings, and alternative suggestions.

Change your plan accordingly. Draft a thorough launch plan. How will the change be announced internally and externally? Employees, stockholders, community leaders, and customers all have different needs for information and different venues for communicating change.

What training is needed internally and externally to explain the change and help others adjust to the change?

What is the grace period for the change to be fully implemented? To protect the relationship (this guiding principle was discussed in Chapter 9), change should not have to happen overnight. Remember, something as simple as our local movie theater changing to a cash-only theater took months to implement. Signs were posted in the lobby. The change was noted in their weekly ad. The ticket cashiers mentioned it with each transaction leading up to the official change date. It was not something the theater took lightly. Movie patrons had to get used to carrying cash in their pockets to see movies. They could no longer simply carry a checkbook.

What key messages does everyone on staff need to know? Don't forget to include *why* something is changing. That was one of our lessons in the guiding principle Communicate clearly and concisely. How often can that be communicated in print, face to face, on the answering machine, etc.?

What customers or employees can give testimonials or show support? When we launched our new career plan, we had leaders from all levels of the field talk about their thoughts on the plan and how it would impact their business and the consultant base as a whole. We even had some who admitted on stage in front of our entire leadership base that they were skeptical at first but have since realized that the changing plan was the right thing to do.

What is your exit strategy? Expect the best, but always plan for the worst. If your change truly is a bad change, how do you go about fixing it? Think back to when Coca-Cola decided to offer New Coke in 1985. Coke decided to offer New Coke after the Pepsi Challenge indicated that more consumers preferred the sweeter taste of their product. Traditional Coke drinkers rejected the new, sweeter version of their old favorite. One loyal customer was quoted as saying that New Coke tasted like it had been left out with the cap off. It was flat.

Despite the research to create a new taste, the packaging to give a new look, and the advertising and promotional dollars that went into the launch, Coca-Cola had to react to overwhelming consumer complaint. Within 90 days of the introduction, Coke admitted it was wrong and reintroduced Coca-Cola Classic. Obviously, the change to

New Coke was not a good one. Now consumers celebrate their love and loyalty to Coca-Cola Classic.

While 90 days is a short window in product and program development, it was definitely not a knee-jerk reaction on Coca-Cola's part.

The bottom line with this guiding principle is don't be afraid to take action. Take action with due diligence. Let the change run its course. Change is hard. Change can be good. People simply need time to adjust.

CHAPTER 13

ENSURE SUSTAINABILITY

❧────────❧

Creative Memories is responsible for making decisions and investments that ensure company and sales force strength and viability today and in the future.

The long-term sustainability of Creative Memories is of utmost importance for our consultants, our customers, and our employee-owners.

We have been teaching millions of people around the world a new way of life, a new tradition, and we don't want to see that end.

Rhonda and my vision all those years ago was that one day everyone who had pictures developed (or, these days, downloaded and printed) would immediately think to place those photographs in an album and document their stories. We are accomplishing this, and we have so much more to do as new generations begin to see the value in documenting their special stories.

We must ensure our sustainability for our current generations of consultants, album makers, and employee-owners as well as those who have yet to join in.

We can achieve this goal by being true to our mission, vision, and guiding principles. We must be true to our brand. And we must commit to having the right processes and people in place to carry us forward.

MISSION, VISION, PRINCIPLES

Our success is driven by three main focuses: our mission, our brand, and our guiding principles. These areas define who we are, the type of organization we pride ourselves on being, and what aspects of our business and identity should stay the same as we change and evolve for the future.

First and foremost there is our mission. Our mission gives us something to believe in; it gives us a common purpose. Our mission of teaching the value of preserving the past, enriching the present, and inspiring hope for the future is what defines Creative Memories. There's an old saying that suggests a hurricane can be traced all the way back to a flap of the wings of a single butterfly. Whether or not that is the case, I do know this: The incredible series of events that have occurred in our history can be traced all the way back to the passion, the commitment, and the belief in the heart of each and every one of our consultants and employee-owners. We believe in what we do. We believe in our mission.

One thing you can't help but notice as you enter our building is our mission statement. It stands outside our front door with the words carved literally into an 8-foot-high piece of granite. And that's only fitting, since those words are the foundation of everything we do, the bedrock of who we are.

Our mission is what makes us unique. It's our rock. But the way we share the mission is our cornerstone. It was never more evident than after the tragedies of September 11.

I was in the car on my way to work when I learned of the attacks on the World Trade Center. I remember sitting there trying to make sense of what this meant when the radio anchor said everyone was waiting to hear from the president. Oddly enough, it dawned on me at that moment that I, too, was a president, and perhaps the employees, consultants, and customers of our organization needed to hear from me too. Perhaps they wanted guidance or reassurance or just hope that we were in this tragedy together and could support each other. At that moment of crisis and confusion, I turned to our mission and offered the following letter to our consultants and employees.

To our Creative Memories family,

The horrific events of September 11 will undoubtedly redefine who we are as individuals and as a nation.

Our thoughts and prayers are extended to everyone within our borders as well as to families in the world who have been impacted by this tragedy.

While devastating acts of war and terrorism impact almost every continent on a daily basis, we have thrived and prospered—virtually untouched. Now, through our pain, we grow even closer to our global family, understanding the heartache and confusion that come from something we cannot understand.

It is a humbling time. It is a frightening time.

In the wake of this chaos, we must unite. We must not be paralyzed with fear. We must walk with purpose. We must remain calm. We must be thoughtful in our actions even when we feel like being angry and resentful.

By doing so, we inspire hope for the future.

Anthropologist Margaret Meade said, "Never doubt that a small group of thoughtful, committed citizens can change the world. Indeed, that is the only thing that ever has."

While I am not naïve enough to think that by teaching the Creative Memories Mission we will wipe out all that is incomprehensible in the world, we cannot underestimate the power of what we do. We help people recognize and cherish all that is important in their lives. For some, we even help work through their grief.

Robert Kennedy used to say, "Some men see things as they are and say why. Others see what could be and say why not." And, in the coming days, I see an important role for us. I truly believe the reflecting, humanizing power of our Mission can play a part in helping heal and restore normalcy.

The human spirit is more powerful than any forces made by man. You help strengthen that spirit. You give the world hope. Please remember these things as you and those around you seek to understand what has happened and offer prayer for us all.

In the weeks following September 11, our consultants and customers united on the Albums of Honor project. The goal of this project was to ensure that anyone who lost someone in the attacks would have an album to document what happened and memorialize their loved one. Our consultants and other album makers reached out with page layouts expressing support, compassion, and love for a nation in shock and grief.

Albums were created and sent from every state in the country and from Australia, Asia, Canada, Europe, and South America. Enough albums were made for every firefighter, police officer, and other workers and their children as well as families affected by the tragedy. Albums went to the large corporations who lost hundreds of their valued employees. Albums were sent to local military outlets and emergency response teams pledging support and gratitude for all that they do. We also collected pages and created four albums that we sent to the White House as a lasting reminder of this tragedy and of how a nation united during a time of great need and supported each other and our first family.

The importance of our mission was never more evident than after September 11, 2001. All of us—each and every one of us who make up the Creative Memories family—are honored by the fact that we've built a company that provides hope, one memory at a time.

Our mission, and the passion and commitment our consultants and employee-owners have for fulfilling that mission, will keep us focused for generations to come. That passion and commitment will sustain us. The importance of preserving memories will not change. The manner in which we preserve them may change as technology changes; nonetheless, people will always have a need to remember who they are, how they live, and what they value. Society will always have a need to remember, celebrate, and connect.

Our second main focus for sustainability is our brand. Our mission is our purpose; our brand is how we are perceived. Creative Memories created the scrapbooking industry. As the industry grew, the time came to shift away from building an industry to differentiating ourselves from the rest of the scrapbooking industry.

In 2003, scrapbooking was the third most popular craft after cross-stitching and home décor painting. It is important that we position ourselves, and our brand, as more than a craft. A craft will fade, a tradition will not. Creative Memories is a tradition.

We have a very strong brand, based on the quality of the products and services we provide. This is why we continue to grow despite the increased retail competition. The service we provide is noticed and valued by consumers. It keeps them coming back to us, relying on us to motivate and inspire them to complete their albums, and trusting us that the quality of our product is unmatched.

The scrapbook albums and supplies sold through the retail market generated an estimated $1.5 to $2 billion in 2003. These sales include every magnetic page album, every plastic album, every scrapbook album, and every type of paper, punches, and other decorative enhancements sold through retail channels. Our sales—through the direct-selling method of distribution—represented approximately $400 million in 2003. And our consultants accomplished these sales in one-on-one meetings and in group presentations. They helped others, encouraged others, and shared with them the importance of preserving their memories. They reached millions of people in 2002. And that reach keeps growing. The personalized service they are providing through direct selling is one of the most recognized components of our brand. In a recent brand awareness study, the buying public told us that if Creative Memories were a person, she would be warm, caring, helpful, fun, and important. That is our brand; that is the type of relationship our consultants have with their customers. And, as we discussed earlier, we must do everything we can to protect the relationship. We must maintain it, enhance it, and celebrate. That will help ensure our sustainability.

The final piece that defines who we are at Creative Memories is our guiding principles, which we have explored in this book. These principles have been around since Rhonda and I conceived of this business. They have been the philosophies that have guided our decisions over time.

I am now convinced that our mission, and our brand combined with these principles gives us a solid foundation on which to make good, sound business decisions that align with who we are as an organization and who we want to continue to be. They, too, help ensure our sustainability.

We have to look to our mission, our brand, and our guiding principles and see to it that everyone—each family and every generation—has the pleasure of discovering this vision and of knowing the joy it brings to life.

Every organization should have a clear understanding of who they are and how decisions are made within the organization. This clear understanding of brand, mission, and operating principles provides a foundation for alignment and direction.

Furthermore, every organization should have a vision—the bigger picture of what it is they provide. For example, MedTronic is a leading manufacturer and supplier of medical technology like pacemakers. Their logo includes the transition of a man from the lying position to standing up. MedTronic understands what they do. They don't simply engineer, manufacture, and sell medical technology. They give people the gift of life, strength, and ability.

A woman I know recently started a housecleaning business after she was laid off from a job she held almost 20 years. When she first started, she was bothered by the stigma that she was a "cleaning lady." She didn't hold an office job. She picked up other people's messes. I talked to her about seeing the bigger vision of what she does. She cleans houses for busy people, so they can spend more time with their family and friends during the rare moments they are at home. She is not a housekeeper; she is a giver of time, peace, and comfort. By understanding the higher vision that we contribute to as an organization, we are able to sustain the challenges that growth, change, and maturation provide.

BRICKS AND MORTAR

In addition to the higher-level elements that govern our day-to-day direction, we have the tangible buildings, equipment, and human resources that are essential to sustainability.

We put the finishing touches on our new 316,000-square-foot facility in St. Cloud, Minnesota, in August 2003. The new manufacturing and distribution facility, located only a few miles from the previous facility, provides twice the room and four times the capacity to support an ever-growing business.

Our consultants are breaking records day in and day out. In February 2003, a record 7,800 new consultants joined our field to share the Creative Memories mission. Prior to that, our record was about 4,200 in 1 month.

And, in February 2003, two days in a row, we shattered our old record of lines (products taken from a particular SKU) picked in 1 day. We went from just over 99,000 (in October 2002) to approximately 100,000 and 101,000, respectively. That's a lot of product to ship out the door and get in the hands of album makers in North America. And that was just at our St. Cloud facility.

We also renovated the interior of the Creative Memories home office to a festive, open office environment that encourages collaboration and fun. No offices exist. Regardless of title or job functionality, everyone has the same space.

And that space is easily reconfigured. Because we do not have office walls, we can easily realign a work team's physical space. We can also increase or decrease workstation size to adjust to growth.

The new design is also reminiscent of someone's home, with a fireplace and conference rooms furnished like living rooms and dining rooms. We wanted it to reflect the essence of direct-selling relationships. Since our consultants work with others in their homes, we wanted a homey setting for our work as well.

At the home office and our facilities in St. Cloud, Minnesota; Sparks, Nevada; Richmond, Virginia; and Yellow Springs, Ohio, we are committed to helping our consultants succeed in their businesses for decades to come. We will achieve this by ensuring we have the facilities, capacity, and technology to help "Make it easy" for them to do business and to help "Protect the relationship" by making sure they have quality product and program when they need it. And we will "Operate from least to most" as we expand to ensure we don't outdo ourselves with overhead and unnecessary spending.

PASS THE TORCH

One of the things that I've often said is, "If only Rhonda or I can make this company successful, then we don't have much."

Many people have been able to build companies. To me, the *real sign* of success is when it can go on without you, when you have developed people and positioned the company so that it will be carried successfully into the future.

We are taking the necessary steps to do this. Our guiding principles help ensure that continuity as we teach our new staff why we do the things we do. But we do so much more.

Our training programs help by teaching newcomers about the direct-selling industry and how it is different than the retail sector.

All new employee-owners go through Direct Selling 101, a course that teaches the lessons Alan Luce, of Luce and Associates, outlined in Chapter 11 on our guiding principle Go for the good of the whole. We also talk about how Creative Memories consultants relate to the concepts Alan teaches.

In addition, we encourage employee-owners to get involved in the direct-selling industry by being a sales representative for other companies. (They are not allowed to be Creative Memories consultants because that would be a conflict of interest. They would have too much inside information about new products, programs, and incentives.) By being members of our Direct Selling Club (how appropriately named!), they are committing to being a sales representative for another company for a minimum of 1 year. They are committing to meeting that company's minimum requirements, attending training meetings, and gathering every other month with the club to share.

At the bimonthly meeting of our Direct Selling Club, they share their monthly sales and recruiting activity. They talk about the topic of the month (e.g., about how their company processes returns and about their company's hostess reward program). And they share their frustrations and successes as well as how those can be applied to their job at Creative Memories.

Through this club, our employee-owners learn how our company's processes and policies compare to other direct-selling companies. They also learn firsthand the joys and frustrations of being an independent business owner. This information is then applied to their job responsibility as we work to make it easy to do business for our consultants.

One of our Direct Selling Club members was trying to earn what we call the 90-Day Success Plan. This encourages a fast start to a home-based business in the first 90 days of operation by rewarding for sales levels. With this other company, she needed to have $1,000, $1,500, and $2,000 in sales in her first 30, 60, and 90 days, respectively.

She was able to reach sales of $2,250 in her first 30 days, just over $2,000 between 31 and 60 days, and only $900 in her final 30-day window. Because sales were not counted cumulatively, she did not earn the incentive. Obviously, she was disappointed, but it opened up discussion about what it is that we want to reward.

Other Direct Selling Club members have expressed frustration when events cancel. They know what it is like to have a calendar full of parties—and to be counting on that monthly income—only to have the parties cancelled or rescheduled because of a scheduling conflict with the hostess. Thus, they can relate when our Creative Memories consultants express similar frustration about their business. Our employee-owners can empathize and provide real advice to our field.

One of our club members is establishing quite a large team and is struggling with her full-time job, her personal sales business, and her leadership role. While we may lose her to her direct-selling job, what she has learned and shared with the group provides us with invaluable information so we can understand how to support our field.

And when we are talking with our consultants and hearing their frustrations, we can say with some certainty, "I know firsthand what that is like." You can't teach that empathy and understanding. It has to be experienced.

While members of our general employee population cannot be Creative Memories consultants, we do require some members of our executive and mid-management team to be consultants for a short time, so they understand what the Creative Memories experience is like.

Our COO, Asha Moran, had to be a consultant for 3 months before joining the home office team. And she will tell you what she loved about being a home-based business owner (establishing a business plan, reconciling the books) and what she hated (cold calling). That experience made her better at her job because she has been there and experienced both the success and the frustration.

Jeff Grong, our current vice president of sales, is responsible for the overall growth and productivity of the field. He directs the sales team on training, development, programs like the 90-Day Success Plan, and incentives. He came to us with more than 20 years of sales and development experience with a consumer-direct grocery division in the United States. He served as vice president of sales at a company where he was responsible for compensation, training, and incentives for the $1.5-billion division.

While he had remarkable experience with a similar value-centered sales organization, he was going to experience some differences, and we wanted him to be ready. His previous employer was direct-to-the-consumer; Creative Memories is party plan. His previous sales force was 99 percent male. Creative Memories is 96 percent female. Other differences are more obvious: groceries versus photo albums.

Jeff spent a month as a Creative Memories consultant. He attended training meetings and identified coordinators to schedule and host his first Home Classes.

"After attending a Home Class, I thought of my sister and a friend as coordinators," Jeff said. "I scheduled the class with my sister, and then she left town for 10 days. Then, I contacted my friend; she was interested but was leaving town, too."

Despite the initial stalled momentum, Jeff stuck to the goals he set for his month as a consultant. "I planned to achieve the 30-day success package. And I'm going to sell three of the Memory Keepers

Collections (which are Creative Memories' customer collections—everything you need and more for working on albums) at my first two classes." He did.

Jeff welcomed the opportunity to be in the field for his initial month. "I'm coming into an organization with sales experience but not the experience that this particular sales force has. I can't gain that knowledge behind a desk," he said. "I needed to experience the joys, the frustrations. I didn't have the full experience of being a Creative Memories consultant in 30 days, but I gained a better understanding of how and why we do what we do in the field."

In the last few years, Creative Memories has had to draw on talent from the direct-selling industry for our executive management team to help our organization reach new heights of success. We wanted people who had experience catapulting a multimillion-dollar organization to the next level.

And we had to embrace that new talent, and their ideas, while acclimating to all that defines Creative Memories.

We have done that and will continue to celebrate the best of our past as we move forward. Organizations should realize that they cannot simply remain stagnant, and they will continue to succeed. Celebrate what defines you. In our case, our mission, vision, and principles define us. Preserve that, and look for ways to continually grow and strengthen your organization. This may mean finding new products or services, like the Campbell Soup Company did. This may mean bringing in new people to offer a fresh perspective on your operations. This may also mean grooming your team to carry on under new leadership.

Sometimes people shy away from succession planning because they fear not being needed or they have delusions of being indispensable. As leaders, the greatest gift we can give our companies, our teams, and our consumers is the ability for the success to continue without us. It is amazing what we can accomplish when we don't care who gets the credit.

For me, having stepped out of the day-to-day role at Creative Memories, it's much like watching your youngest child leave the nest.

It's hard; but it's the right thing to do because you want more than anything in the world for that child to flourish on her own. My plan to retire as president of Creative Memories was 5 years in the making. My goal was to ensure that we had the right people and processes in place to carry Creative Memories forward. Incidentally, my comfort level with our people and processes was high enough that I actually retired 2 years earlier than planned. I know that our mission, vision, and guiding principles will guide our organization for generations to come as it seeks out new ways to build on our brand.

Although I am actively involved as a cofounder who speaks at various field events, it was still hard to give up the day-to-day business activity and watch it survive without me. But I had faith that it would thrive without me being there full time because everyone at Creative Memories has worked to ensure sustainability. Our company is alive and well, is flourishing wildly, and is aimed carefully at that future. These guiding principles will help us get there easily, effectively, and successfully.

As I mentioned earlier, all organizations should have guiding principles to drive focused, consistent decision making and to empower the team with understanding and the ability to carry on into the future.

PART III

LEADING INTO THE FUTURE

CHAPTER 14

INSPIRING HOPE
FOR THE FUTURE

❧———————❧

While our guiding principles serve as the foundation for our decision making at the home office, other personal lessons in life can help us all succeed at home and in the office.

BE OPEN TO OTHERS

Nothing great was ever accomplished alone. Other people provide us with expertise, support, friendship, accountability, positive challenges—you name it. And, as my good friend Susan Iida-Pederson says, we are all bigger, better, and brighter because of it. We have so much to learn from each other, and we don't have to learn simply from those whom we know. We should be open to learning from and being inspired by anyone and everyone we meet. As a result, we will achieve great things together.

Keeping relationships alive is important to me. That is why I continually capture them in my keepsake albums.

That is also why in 1994—when I celebrated a rather significant birthday—I decided to bring my Ohio friends together with my Minnesota friends and a cousin from Texas. I called it "The Gathering."

For 4 days, we recharged our souls. I remember hiking through the woods, soaking up the sunshine, and catching up with each other's lives. But most of all, I remember trekking with this group to the Mall of America. I was just beginning chemotherapy at the time for breast cancer and would be in need of a wig shortly. What would have been a discouraging and difficult task became *fun* with my friends.

Imagine four middle-aged women trying on every wig in sight from voluptuous blonde cascades—that made us look like Rapunzel—to spiky little numbers that made us look like punk stars. And imagine the laughter. That is, indeed, what friends are for.

I met some of these good friends through happenstance. And they continually remind me that we can be incredibly blessed both personally and professionally when we reach out to share our journey and embrace those who happen to come into our lives.

Before that can happen, we have to recognize how important it is not to prejudge people. You simply do not know who is being sent to you and why they are being sent to you unless you reach out.

Life simply isn't perfect. If we all received everything that we ever needed in every relationship that we ever had, life would be a snap. Working a business would be a snap. Life doesn't always work that way. If you ever feel that you are not getting the support that you need, I invite you to find that support. It's a chance to grow, to make it happen your way. And it's a chance at ownership. It's an opportunity to look around and figure out how to make life work.

Our Creative Memories consultants reach out to each other and succeed together every day. I loved it when I learned that five of our leaders in Atlanta set up the Atlanta All Stars in 1996, a big meeting for all consultants in the area regardless of whose team they are on. The All-Star mission statement speaks of the "abundance mentality . . . company loyalty . . . and a cooperative and thoughtful spirit." Today, 100 to

150 consultants routinely attend these upbeat, quarterly meetings packed with training, support, and recognition for all. They learn from each other about how to be a successful businessperson and how to balance family and business life. Meetings like this take place all over North America because our consultants recognize the value of being open to others.

In addition to group dynamics, our consultants also pick Pacing Partners. A Pacing Partner is another consultant who will challenge you, offer advice, and hold you accountable to your goals. It's a friendly competitor, somebody to take the journey with.

There's a passage in the Bible that says, "For I was hungry and you gave me food. I was thirsty and you gave me drink. I was a stranger and you welcomed me." There are many versions of this philosophy, in stories and in song. And there are many ways of receiving the blessings of reaching out.

You just never know what wonderful people can come into your life when you are open to receiving them. So don't be afraid to reach out, in all areas of your life, to professional organizations, social groups, coworkers, and friends. The rewards will amaze you.

Remember, you never know what lessons, what enrichment, what meaning can be brought to your life when you connect with others. Be open to others and see what incredible gifts are tucked away behind what may seem to be ordinary moments in time!

BELIEVE IN YOURSELF

There is a quote from Eleanor Roosevelt that I find inspirational and true. She said, "Believe in yourself. You gain strength, courage, and confidence by every experience in which you stop to look fear in the face. You must do that which you think you cannot do."

How many hundreds of times in our lives have we all had to do that? Like many of you, I have raised children. I was home for 11 years raising children. And there was no instruction manual.

I do not think that the world realizes the skill set necessary to raise children well. Collectively, it is the world's most influential position.

Parents shape lives. And parents need endless skill. It has been my observation over the years that parents usually don't realize the skill set that they have developed in their everyday lives of parenting and volunteering.

First of all, parents need the organizational skills of a CEO. Parents, in a single day, need to balance the schedules of three children, a partner, a home, three meals a day—when one child is vegetarian and one child is allergic to all milk products—cleaning, carpools, dancing, flute and karate lessons, orthodontist appointments, parent-teacher meetings, homework sessions that involve tutoring algebra which you *don't* remember, and, oh yes, remembering to schedule a plumber because the kitchen sink just malfunctioned and flooded the family room below.

Did you notice a few necessary time-management skills and resource allocation skills tucked in there? And, of course, as a parent, one must have the negotiating skills of a used-car salesperson and the peace-making skills of Mother Teresa. That is to say nothing of financial skills necessary to balance a budget in a world in which your 17-year-old's senior pictures can cost $1,400.

And if you volunteer, you have experienced moments much like what I fondly compare to "herding cats." If you can organize volunteers, you can organize the next missile launch to outer space. Trust me. If you have volunteered, or managed volunteers, you know *exactly* what I'm talking about.

When I first started Creative Memories, people would say, "Where did you develop the skills to start a company?" I would say, "Raising kids! Being a volunteer!" All of us have been gaining these same skills daily; we should recognize them, be proud of them, and celebrate them. We should also apply what we have learned to the world of work.

We should also overcome fear. We all have our moments, those times when we ask ourselves, "Just exactly how am I going to pull this one off?" When have you asked yourself that? And how did you overcome it?

One way to do it is to face your fears head on. Just tackle them. Don't give up or shy away.

Another tidbit that I think is essential is being resourceful. Never say no to opportunity. Figure out a way. There are so many resources in this world—coaches, experts on everything under the sun, books, articles, and Web sites. There are so many people out there to help you along the way if you just don't "do yourself in" by saying no before you even try.

Sometimes we also simply need to act the part. We need to fake it until we make it.

I have learned many things over the years:

- Respect the skills one develops as a parent, and as a volunteer.
- Overcoming fear and never saying no to opportunity has opened many doors.
- Resources are plentiful and available for the asking.
- There are moments in life when one needs to wing it momentarily, to act the part.
- Inner strength is an amazing gift.

WORK ON YOUR OWN ALBUMS

Being president and cofounder of Creative Memories has not been easy. And I'm not referring to the day-to-day business challenges.

When you are the leader of the scrapbooking pioneer, you are under pressure to complete your photo albums. While I actively work on my albums, up until the last few years, I was overwhelmed by the *activity* of album making.

Then, something happened to me that helped me cross over into another dimension of album making. I went from the *activity of* album making to the *emotion in* album making.

This happened because of my Uncle Paul, my mother's oldest brother. Paul was stationed in Louisiana before he served in the Pacific in World War II. He met his wife, Hyacinth, there. She was a beautiful, spunky little woman. They were married over 50 years and blessed with six children.

Many years ago, Hyacinth was diagnosed with Alzheimer's disease. For 7 or 8 years, Uncle Paul took care of her. He had to be there for her every minute. In October 2001, Hyacinth died.

I went back to Ohio for the funeral and took a heritage album that I had been working on to share with Uncle Paul. When he came to a photograph of Hyacinth and him before the war, he stopped talking and just stared at the picture. Then he said out loud sort of to himself in a whisper, "She *was* a cute little thing, wasn't she?"

He just stared at the picture, and it brought him back to a whole different world. Despite all that had happened in 50 years of marriage, he was instantly transported back to that moment, to feeling those same emotions as if it were yesterday. It was so sweet. It was *so touching*. All he could remember was falling in love with Hyacinth.

We remember through photos. We feel emotion. We feel love, apprehension, loss. We feel butterflies in our stomach. That is the phenomenal power of our albums! That is what takes us from the activity of album making to the emotion of album making.

My mother's photos were in drawers. Endless drawers.

When I inherited those photographs, I inherited what I first saw as an activity to accomplish. I had to get heritage albums done. I became wrapped up in the mechanics of album making. I had to sort, organize, hunt down historical information, make reprints of some one-of-a-kind photos. I had to get the project done.

But, while completing these activities, I discovered emotion and understanding because of the insight I gained from that short visit with my Uncle Paul.

My Irish grandmother, Grace Elizabeth McCafferty, was a major influence in my life. I was the first grandchild and could easily walk the few blocks to my grandparents' home.

My grandmother was named Grace; and, she lived her life by grace and goodness. She is the one who taught me, "If you do the right things, for the right reasons, the right things will happen." Her beautiful spirit, her forgiveness, her acceptance of people moved me. *It moves me still*, and she has been gone for 34 years.

Like everyone else, I imagine, I started my heritage album because it is the thing to do. But as I gazed at the pictures of my grandparents as a young, engaged couple, I couldn't help but get caught up in the emotion of their story! I don't know about you, but I just thought of these people as my grandparents. I didn't spend a lot of time thinking about their lives, the emotions they felt, how they lived.

As I worked on my heritage album, I came to more clearly understand my mother, too. She had an amazing spirit.

I came across her grade cards. And I love her grades:

- Obeys signals promptly: Unsatisfactory.
- Walks and talks quietly: Unsatisfactory.
- Is courteous in speech and manner: Unsatisfactory.
- Uses time well: Improving.

When I was showing this to someone at home office, she said, "Oh Cheryl, now I understand *you* a little bit better!"

I will point out that in the same 6 weeks on my mom's grade cards, she earned 5 B's and 3 A's. And by the second 6 weeks, all the U's had become S's. That grade card told me so much about my mother's spirit.

I have photos of my mother with a man named Earl on the corner of Limestone and Mulberry in Springfield, Ohio. On the back, it was labeled: summer of '42. I also have V-letters sent to her from a soldier named Bill. He'd write, "Hello Sweetheart, How's my girl today . . ." These were also dated the summer of '42.

The girl in these photographs, the girl who received these letters, these grades, she wasn't *only* my mother. She was young, flirtatious, and fun. She loved life. She had spirit. This was my mom before marriage, before kids, before responsibility.

And I may not have recognized this, had I not been working on my albums and started looking for the emotion in the stories. The depth. The meaning.

I could tell stories forever about how the emotions tied to album making have warmed my heart! They have helped me understand and appreciate all that I have.

The book, *A Tree Full of Angels*, says, "Glory comes streaming from the table of ordinary life." I love that thought! And I truly believe that when we capture and elevate the ordinary little moments of life in our albums that we add a sheen, a glory to our existence unlike any other. Because in the end, all those little ordinary moments, humble though they may be, all together create our eternities.

But I want to share one last album that is near and dear to my heart. My mother died in 2001. Six months before she died, she had been up to see me. And we had a grand time. One night at our local college the St. Cloud State Women's Basketball team declared her their honorary coach. And let me tell you, this athletic and determined woman was in her glory. She was on the court, in the locker room, on the bench advising the players. She was everywhere, and she was having a ball!

An album was made of that night. Albums speak volumes.

Six months later, Mother ended up in the hospital with cancer. There she was in bed, her pale face in a sea of white sheets, wearing a white hospital gown with her nearly white hair having not been done in weeks. She—and her pizzazz—were lost.

Well, there was a young doctor on duty who had never before met my mother. He told me, "Well, with people this age, we usually don't do much treatment." Immediately, instinctively, I got out of my chair, darted into her room, brought out that album that showed her delighting in her coaching glory, opened it wide, and said, "Now *this* is who we're talking about."

I must tell you now that I don't worry so much about how people will judge my pages. I just want to get my pictures on the page and my stories told. I find much more joy in discovering the emotion of the stories than the satisfaction of completing a perfect page.

Albums are powerful. Albums dignify and honor those we love and heighten our understanding both of them and ourselves. Albums celebrate and validate human lives. Albums capture the quiet glory of ordinary moments that define our existence. Albums can lift us all to an emotional place.

In the hustle and bustle of this big old noisy world we live in, it is key that we stay connected with what matters most in our lives, the extraordinary moments of everyday life. Regardless of the money we make, businesses we build, and accomplishments we add to our resume, our lives are measured in precious moments.

HAVE FUN

In life and in business, we can get so busy that we forget to have fun. My philosophy has always been: Don't take yourself too seriously. As long as life goes on, we are still breathing, and the sun is going to come up tomorrow, we'll be okay.

That doesn't mean that life won't have its challenges. When we enjoy life and look for the value in fun, we can overcome those challenges. All that I've accomplished or accumulated is great; but if it's all gone tomorrow, I can get a job waiting tables and live in a studio apartment. As long as I can keep my family, my photo albums, and my puppies with me, everything else is just stuff.

So, how can you have fun? Any number of ways, really. Sometimes it simply means getting to know the people you work with. In Creative Memories' early days when all of us would be out on the distribution floor packing boxes to get them out the door, we'd have fun singing and telling jokes. We often said we could work 60 hours a week as long as it was fun. Who even wants to work 20 hours a week in a job that is not enjoyable?

During training meetings, we've been known to take a stretch break by leading line dancing or teaching the chicken dance. We've given meeting attendees bubbles to blow or beach balls to toss around. Some of our departments go out on the lawn and throw the football or flying discs around during break. There are so many things you can do personally and professionally to lighten things up a bit.

Believe it or not, we broke ground on our home office in December, in Minnesota, when the temperature was below zero. At our weekly management meeting, we were discussing the groundbreaking ceremony, and a few people actually suggested that we shouldn't have one because it would be so cold. That just isn't part of our nature, though. So we invited all the local government officials and employees to the ceremony. We were bundled up. I was wearing antlers, and we gathered for a very cold, but memorable photo. Then we went inside for hot chocolate and speeches.

One year, for our holiday party, we opted to convert our construction site to a winter wonderland (no, our fun doesn't always revolve around construction, but we've had a lot of it, and have had to make it fun). Amidst the gypsum panel, concrete, and metal, we ate, danced, and celebrated.

There's so much you can do. Roll around on the floor with kids. Have a date night each week with your significant other. Take the time to tell a joke (but make it appropriate for work or family). Have birthday treats at work. And don't forget to dress up.

Halloween is my favorite holiday, and I always dress up. When I first started at The Antioch Company it was close to Halloween, and I asked everyone what they would be wearing to work to celebrate. Very few people responded. I showed up on Halloween as the Wicked Witch of the West and gave out candy. I was the only one who dressed up.

Now, at Creative Memories, every year we have a Halloween costume contest and parade, so employees who dress up can parade through the home office and manufacturing facility to show off their costumes.

We have Family Day each year, so our employees can bring their families to eat and play at our facility. Sometimes we'll even put management in a dunk tank just for fun.

On our company's milestone anniversaries, the creative services department always makes me a hat to wear. It usually stands a few feet off my head and takes some balance, but the hat proudly boasts our number of years. And I wear it with pride.

Dressing up transcends Halloween, too. Every other year, our Winter Seasons party invites employees and their guests to dress up. We've had a renaissance theme, fifties theme, boogie wonderland theme, and more.

Having fun is part of our corporate values, and I'd like to think that I played a small part in that. In fact, on a rather significant birthday of mine not too long ago, I came to work only to be greeted by hundreds of Cheryl Lightles. People wore red wigs and big earrings and tried to mimic my manner of dress.

Once you've become a costume, you know you've arrived.

Index

About the Authors

Cheryl Lightle is cofounder of Creative Memories, a $500 million direct-selling business specializing in photo-safe scrapbook albums and album-making accessories. The company has more than 90,000 consultants in nine countries, has been featured in numerous television, radio, and print media, and has won the Creating Keepsakes Readers' Choice Award for five years in a row.

Heidi L. Everett overseas community relations and is the company historian for Creative Memories.